AF295254

By P. H. TELL

TUNING BRAINWAVES ON THE
WINGS OF ADVENTURE

Kustantaja: BoD – Books on Demand, Helsinki, Suomi

Valmistaja: BoD – Books on Demand, Norderstedt, Saksa

ISBN: 9789523188228

TABLE OF CONTENTS

On the border of practical awareness, we lived our lives in our world. Nevertheless, we sometimes reached the coronary of life's ultimate origin, and looked at the open scenery of endless consciousness with amazement.

CHAPTER ONE

Two pairs of binoculars were following when a tall, light-brown-haired man in green clothes floated down with the help of a rainbow-colored parachute. Gravity took him lower fast, while the parachute let him feel as if he were flying a bit so he could direct his landing. The light of the sun was vanishing and giving space to the pale half-moon. The man seemed to disappear somewhere between a forest and a stony square where some bushes were growing.

The spectator who was farther away waved to his mate, who was already sitting on his moped. Nearby, another watcher, a youngster who'd climbed up an old tree, began to find his way down where an older woman waited for him with a warm smile.

Olav Wave didn't notice his observers; he concentrated on landing. When he touched the ground, his heart jumped with excitement an extra beat because he hoped to be closer to rescuing Sophia, wherever she was.

Olav's thoughts already had been partly with Sophia for a while, a marvelous friend and colleague whom he'd arrived to search for.

Sophia'd sent one message before her phone seemed to stop working. She'd texted that if there weren't signs of her, Hira Karmala could help.

Olav had tried to reach Sophia ever since; such a message could leave anyone feeling worried. He'd contacted Hira and simply said that he would arrive. He'd been on a work trip in Delhi, so this wasn't too long of a curve to do, especially when his friends had given him a private flight to this area.

Here he now was, wondering if he'd rushed and exaggerated his worries for Sophia. Anyway, he had taken his leave. "A hilarious holiday indeed," he mumbled.

He'd managed to injure his ankle a bit when he landed with the parachute. Although there was mild pain in the ankle, he didn't believe that it would get worse. But it was now troubling him more and radiating toward his calf.

Olav sat down on a gray, hard stone. Simultaneously, behind him, ran a young, dark-haired boy with a big, friendly smile; gray shirt; and trousers. With him was an ageless-looking woman in a long, green sari and long-sleeved, blue blouse. She wore a blue scarf on her head. Olav turned around with amazement when the woman spoke to him in English.

"Namaste," she said. "You are far away from home. Thank you for arriving! I am Sophia's Aunt Shilpa Karmala, and this is her cousin Ravi."

"Oh, namaste," Olav said. "So Sophia found you after all! I am surprised, since there was so little information about her adoption and biological family. How did you find me?"

"You'd sent your arrival date and some hints to Hira, my daughter's husband, and we have been keeping our eyes open with Ravi." Shilpa smiled.

"That's great. I'm very glad to see you. And where is Hira?" Olav massaged his ankle.

"I'll tell you all about that later. Now, do you have pain in your ankle? May I look?"

Olav stretched his left leg, and Shilpa took a grip of his ankle. "No bone is broken. I can remove the pain, if you let me, so that we can walk forward. Are you familiar with energy healing?"

"I know that there have been people among the indigenous population who knew this skill. In those cultures, that kind of skill is natural, even if the terms describing the structures of human material are not defined by physics. Personally, I could say that in theory it means that a healing energy streaming from a person's hands to the injured spot can take place until the layers of muscles, molecules, atoms, and particles are like those in a healthy body."

"I couldn't agree more, but I would add that the will and concentration of the healer are cornerstones." Shilpa held his ankle. Her black eyes concentrated, and her mouth was a firm line. "So try to step on this foot now, please."

Olav felt a hot stream on the painful spot. He stood and looked at Shilpa, smiling. "Ooh, unbelievable. It's different to experience than to have a theory. Thanks a million!' He shouted joyfully.

Yet one question was burning his heart the most, so he continued. "Now, tell me, where do you think Sophia has disappeared? I got her last message when

I was in Delhi, and in that message she asked me to contact Hira if anything strange happens. I thought that the message arose more questions than answers, and the total silence afterward was strange enough for me."

"Maybe you also have a hunch for an adventure." Shilpa laughed mysteriously. "Let's walk to the house while we talk. The darkness will soon land, and I'd rather be inside the house in this area."

Ravi went, almost dancing a few steps ahead them.

Olav looked at them with worried, warm, golden-brown eyes under his eyebrows and hurried his steps. "What's going on? Tell me." His voice was low but firm. But he would have to wait for an answer.

They walked in silence on dry soil between big stones for a while. Dust flew in the air under their steps.

Shilpa began to talk. "She found us, which was a big, pleasant shock to all. We'd thought that she died or, if somehow she'd survived the bus accident, became a victim of human trafficking, as so many do. Oh, how I despise the slavery of our time, even if I think that more slaves are the ones who misuse other people. They are slaves of their own desires. They are weakest of all weak when they give their humanity away. What would give them back self-respect, which is a twin brother of respecting other people's lives?" Shilpa's voice was filled with frustration.

She continued more peacefully. "Anyway, with Sophia, we caught up with each other about our lived lives and discussed a lot. Toward the end of her visit, she learned a significant secret of our family. I assumed, based on my impressions on her that she was ready to hear about it. I am afraid that it can be the reason for her disappearance."

"What secret?" Olav had bad exceptions.

They approached a big bush when Ravi suddenly turned around and put his finger on his lips, showing the others to stop behind the bush. They hadn't yet switched any torch on, which seemed now a fortunate coincidence.

It was rather dim, despite the half-moon. Olav, Shilpa, and Ravi stayed as silent as possible behind the bush. Olav then heard a previously agreed-upon signal that sounded like a rusty night bird.

Shilpa, Olav, and Ravi froze where they stood, holding their breaths and trying to locate where the sound came from. Trusting the dimness, Olav tried to check who was making the sound, for he already had Hira's mother-in-law and grandson as guides.

The multilimbed bush was beside them; at first, they couldn't see anyone through it. Then, little by little, after slowly moving their necks, they saw someone was standing about fifty meters away.

They realized with nervousness that, without the leaves, that person would've seen them, too. They noticed, even in the weak light, that the person's head shone a bit—as sweating, bare skin will do—and the man was small and fat.

Shilpa, Olav, and Ravi looked in the dim light at each other and kept their tongues. They tried to breathe as quietly as possible and wait to see what the man would do next.

After making the strange birdcall ten times, the man murmured with anger and waved to someone. Olav saw a rather long, stick-like thing in the hands of the other, bigger man who approached the angry one. The stick reflected light as if it were metal. Maybe it was a gun.

After what seemed to be hours to the hiders, the two men apparently became too bored to wait any longer. They disappeared behind trees in the distance.

Ravi smiled, encouraging Olav to flash his own white teeth. They all began to run.

The sand crunched under their feet. They had to switch their lamps on to see where to step. Their breaths got heavy, but they continued the escape. After they crested a hill, Olav could see a house.

It had one floor and a flat roof. From its two windows, light shone from behind thin curtains. Because there were no other houses nearby and the next light came from much farther away, Olav rationalized to himself that it was their destination.

Ravi and Shilpa pushed Olav quickly inside the house. They all had to blink several times to get used to the lamplight inside the room. Ten pairs of eyes stared at them curiously. One pair—blue, to Olav's astonishment—belonged to Sophia's grandpa and foster father, Leevi.

Leevi, a middle-size, slim, white-haired man, stood up and came to shake Olav's hand. The elder man's head was on the level Olav's armpit, and Olav bent his head to take a good look into the sky-blue eyes. Leevi said in playful voice, "Welcome, Olav, Sophia's friend. Shilpa and Ravi found you easily, I guess."

Ashmita, a woman about Olav's age, was sitting in the middle of the room with a baby in her arms. They were surrounded by children of different ages. All had big, dark eyes; beautiful faces; and nice, ethnic clothes. The mother and the girls had pink tops with short sleeves and blue-and-green skirts with small, red-and-yellow patterns. The boys had all-white shirts and pants. Olav assumed that the family had celebrated something during that day. He felt embarrassed and hoped that they had not dressed up because of his arrival. He was not at his best, with minimal luggage and a simple, green jacket and trousers, which were now dusty.

Olav considered the people inside wonderful. He concentrated on counting them and let his body to calm down after the stress of running. They were four girls and five boys, Ravi included.

Shilpa smiled proudly and told the woman something, using her hands to describe more lively. Olav concluded that the woman was Hira's wife, for she lifted her worried eyes to Olav and began to speak slowly and carefully, using English. "You are very welcome!"

They all sat on the large, red, soft carpet, which had yellow, decorative patterns. Olav enjoyed the colors of the cozy room. The curtains had sweet, little, red flowers on white, and the walls were warm orange. On the side table were pictures of Hindu gods—a dancing Shiva; a calm, blue Krishna; a beautiful, black-haired Sarasvati—but also pictures of a Buddha in the lotus pose surrounded by a green aura and a Christ with open arms, a halo, and pale rays radiating from around his whole body. Olav looked at the bookshelf and recognized several books of those religions, as well as Jainism and a Koran.

Olav asked a question to confirm what he believed had happened. "Was Hira in a car accident?"

Ashmita and Shilpa nodded. "He hit his head," Ashmita said.

"Is he still at the hospital?" Olav was concerned how serious the situation in this family was.

"He is still in the local hospital. A car that passed his donkey had, for some reason, made the animal wild." Ashmita hugged her baby as she lived through the news again. "Hira was thrown to the ground. He'd hit his head and was unconscious when he was found. He gets best possible care. My mother, Shilpa, happens to work in that hospital occasionally, even if she is on pension."

The door opened, and a man of Leevi's size but even thinner stepped in. His turban was white, and his light-blue shirt and trousers looked as if they'd just arrived from the wash. His face was angry at first, but he turned his lips to a small smile. He told the little girls to get up from the soft carpet where they sat. He sat there, and the girls sprang into another room. Olav and Leevi looked at the newcomer, wondering at the familiar way he treated the family. Hira's wife, Ashmita, introduced them and explained that he was her older brother Rajan.

Shilpa looked at Rajan with suspicion. "My son is the person who saw Sophia last. He was supposed to guide her, but he kept saying that Sophia just insisted to be left alone at the most exciting point of the route. I should have guided her myself, but I trusted my son." There was a tinge of accusation but also regret in her voice.

CHAPTER TWO

A day earlier…

Rajan hadn't spoken many words since they left by his noisy, brown Land Cruiser. He had driven skillfully on narrow roads, avoiding holes and big stones on the way. He had knotted his black eyebrows and stared at the road in deep concentration. A turban covered his long, black hair. The radio had been on the whole time, and Sophia's ears under her dark, thick hair were singing. She didn't understood many of the words, but the music was relaxing. Rajan braked firmly and turned the car to an open, flat area in the middle of a small pine forest.

A single black bear with a white V shape on his chest looked at them till he decided to turn toward the forest. He began to run when the approaching noise of a helicopter frightened him.

Rajan noticed the animal and began to yell with excitement. "I should have been quicker! I can make good money off the gall bladder and skin if I sell them in India, you see!"

Sophia was astonished at Rajan's reaction. "He's beautiful. I think they are rare and vulnerable spices."

He turned to speak to her. "They can be dangerous. You would be the fragile one if you face them. Look there. Up on the tree is his nest-like building."

Sophia saw a structure made of branches somewhere in the middle of a tree. Then the landing helicopter covered her view.

"So shall I start my walkabout from here?" Sophia felt excited.

"Now," said Rajan. "You will be given a flight all the way to the beginning of the route."

"Seriously? OK. I wondered a bit about the price of all this, but a helicopter flight explains a lot." Sophia laughed. "I am grateful that Hira, Ashmita, and my aunt, your mother, welcomed me warmly. We got very close in a short time."

She lifted her big rucksack out from the car without waiting for Rajan to do it. She thought it might have been too heavy, but it was better to be prepared, for she wasn't sure what to expect. She'd packed her simple climbing equipment along with a light sleeping bag, a small tent, and food stuff.

They stepped in a dark-green helicopter. The pilot showed them how to fasten their seat belts and use earpieces.

Sophia wanted to keep on speaking, so they were shouting to each other over the noise of engine. "Rajan, you have helped me so much. I'm afraid that no money I paid for this will ever compensate you!" She suspected he hadn't told her everything. "Do you have some final advice for me?"

"Maybe." He turned his eyes away from her scrutinizing stare.

The trip by car had been exhausting. She'd slept at first, and then they'd just driven without any pause for some hours. Now it was afternoon, and she held her breath when looking the scenery.

Rajan pointed toward the peaks. "As you see, there are the peaks of Api and Nampa in the south-facing slopes of the Himalayas. They are the origins of the Seti River." He continued like a travel guide. "The borders of India and China, the area of Tibet, meet Nepal's in that area. In that direction is Mount Kailash, the origin of the longest rivers in Asia, like Indus, Brahmaputra River, and Karnali River."

"So beautiful. There is the conservation area of Api Nampa. Wasn't it established in 2010? Impressive! And no wonder that Mount Kailash is the holy place of Bon, Buddhism, Hinduism, and Jainism. The mountains command deep respect. I can't find any words to describe all this."

Rajan seemed to lose interest, so Sophia changed topics. "Are there many wild animals in the place where you'll leave me?"

"Dear cousin, you don't have to face hungry tigers or leopards or walk sweating through subtropical vegetation areas. Of course, I cannot guarantee that you won't meet any nasty predators—animal or human. But not many other tourists usually find their way there, since we are not going to that kind of route."

"That's a scary matter to say about human predators, since for animals it's natural to hunt for eating, but for human beings to ambush each other…that is, in my opinion, a nasty choice."

"Do not worry. You can determine what happens to you by avoiding certain areas. The human predators tend to destroy each other sooner or later. Anyway, I'll take good care of you. You know that I can even negotiate a good marriage to you. After all, you are a relative. Then your husband would take care of you." He winked. Then he turned his head and looked out the window.

Sophia enjoyed the view through the window. Below them, lively villages looked like animated paintings. The scenery of colorful, snow-capped mountains under a setting sun was amazing and touched her heart with humility.

"Rajan, has your mother spoken about individuals who could see more broadly? They had a bird's-eye perspective above the prevailing culture and society as we now have over mountains."

"Sure she has, but those people are rare. To you and me, they are only a dream."

Sophia didn't care about the hopeless tune of Rajan's voice. She was enthusiastic. "Some people have a kind of similar pure beauty and strength like these mountains. Shilpa told that there were many modest, brave people who could use their breathing during meditation to purify ignorance from the world and send out truth instead. A huge task, and still they carried on with it. How could they have that kind of courage among a hostile and fearful majority?"

Rajan smiled ironically. "We all have our place; no more, no less. We would be too weak to carry out such a task in one life. To try to take care of one's own family is enough, or even to care oneself sometimes." He sounded sad.

But Sophia had no time to find out more because the pilot gave them a sign, and questions sank somewhere into the background of Sophia's mind.

Rajan looked at her with pity. "From now on, Sophia, you are on your own. You can come back with me if you like, as you see the route is straight up this cliff wall."

"Thank you so much, Rajan. I appreciate this!" Sophia's voice was still filled with enthusiasm; she was about to begin the final stage of opening the mystery her aunt had told her about. "Will you meet me here, say, after two days?"

"Sure, as you see here is hardly a signal for a mobile phone, so I still advise you to return now with me. Here can be dangerous! You can still decide not to go." He saw Sophia's determined face and continued. "After two days, I'll come back, and you better be in the valley and give a sign. My free advice is that you stay in the valley. I think that climbing up is too much for you."

Then Rajan seemed to come to a conclusion, and he sounded impatient. "If you manage to climb up, check the waterfall carefully, and you will maybe find the last part of the route. Remember, here things move and live. There is not much unchangeable on this shakable continent." He sighed.

Sophia gave him a friendly smile, took her rucksack, and jumped the short distance from the helicopter to the ground. When her feet touched the sand, she began to run away from the air current of the rotors.

The sky was clear, and Sophia's spirit was high with adrenaline and excitement, but she was sensible. Time had passed since Rajan had kindly shown her the mountains. Now she considered it wise to set up a camp.

The surroundings were attractive and fascinating. Three yaks came to her sight to eat the green grass. The wind was soft on her face, and its humming sound in the tops of the pines gave her a peaceful feeling. She decided to take photos with her travel-sized Leica camera as long as there was enough light.

A Himalayan monal stepped on the grass. His long, metallic-green crest and coppery feathers on his back and neck shined in the sun as he flew away.

Red flowers were blossoming in their beauty, and Sophia guessed that they were rhododendrons. They reminded her so much of the flowers that she had on her windowsill back home.

She could have stared at the snow-capped mountains around her for ages. Reaching heights touched her inner yearning. Was the truth unreachable or just behind an unlocked space in herself?

She tried to remember what the mountains and red flowers reminded her about. Then she knew: a discussion with Olav in Zurich.

"Sophia, have you ever thought how the human brain is such a wonderful machine?" Olav looked at her when the traffic light was red.

"What do you mean exactly? I use my machine every day with amazement. You see, I tune my brain waves almost as eagerly as you." Sophia was joking.

"Well, for example, special skills or exceptional memory."

"Oh, you mean situations when some autistic geniuses express exact numbers they'd observed, remember thousands of books they'd read, or list past dates on calendars. Or people who can play music without any mistakes just by listening to it once. How do you explain that?" Sophia enjoyed challenging him.

Olav looked at Sophia, who sat next to him in small electric car in the middle of Zurich's lively traffic. The traffic light was already changing to green. "That's due to the different uses of the brain. Usually, the left side doesn't disturb a person in those cases as much. That allows the right side of the brain to notice details."

Olav turned the wheel and drove the car in a parking place. "Let's go for coffee somewhere. There. Can you see that terrace with the big, red flowers like azaleas on the sides?" He pointed at an inviting cafeteria in a building made of red-brown wood.

In the terrace, they sat to discuss. Sophia took a slice of Sachertorte chocolate cake with apricot jam. Later, she would recall the delicious taste of black chocolate and the aroma of strong coffee. "Zurich seems so wealthy of a place and very multinational, too," she said. "But to continue our discussion about borders and possibilities of the human brain, what about brain activities in sleep or near death?"

Olav tasted his Irish coffee. "Mmm. Anyone can reach broader levels of observation during those states. It's quite common that during a sleep, time has no limits, especially the future, which can reveal parts of itself."

"How?" Sophia looked at his fine profile. His mouth was serious, and his warm eyes were like golden honey.

"For instance, a person has a repetitive dream about another person whom she'll meet later or about a situation that will happen when she's awake. Sometimes, dreams have even saved lives after a person has received the warning while sleeping." Olav noticed some chocolate on the side of her upper lip. With a natural gesture, he wiped it away.

A feeling of hunger returned Sophia's mind back to her camp. She decided to eat as properly as possible. She took her Trangia, a gas burner for cooking, and prepared her vegetable soup with cheese.

She had to walk fifty meters forward and follow powerful noise to find water for her bottle. She was almost sure that it was the same waterfall she would meet once she climbed up. She sank her bottle under the ice-cold water.

CHAPTER THREE

Olav was wondering how to react to everything. He felt overwhelmed.

He looked at Leevi, who, despite his age, was in good condition. "Leevi, why did you arrive here? Didn't you know that I shall search for Sophia? It can be dangerous for you to wander around. After all, you are not a youngster."

Leevi looked at him with a tiny smile. "Sophia is very important to me, too. In her message to me, she mentioned Hira Karmala and told about Shilpa. I was so excited and curious that I booked a trip before she disappeared so that I could get to know her mother's biological relatives. As you said, I'm beginning to have fewer years ahead of me than behind me, so there is no time to waste. All moments are precious! Here I am now, and I will come with you to search for her."

Shilpa'd observed both Olav and Leevi with clever eyes. "Now we shall eat!"

She added in Nepalese language some words toward a curtain, which the two older girls had gone behind when their uncle arrived. The girls stepped in, carrying steaming bowls.

Delicious, exotic aromas filled the room. Olav recognized the fragrances of garlic, ginger, and cinnamon.

The atmosphere was slightly tense, so Olav decided to behave as his usual self. He was curious and wanted to comment about the different religious decorations in the house. "What is the core of all religion? You must be quite an expert, since I couldn't help noticing all these pictures and books."

Shilpa looked at him and laughed. "Very good question. But tell me first, what do you exactly have in mind?"

Olav felt satisfied to continue, because this was one of his favorite topics. "As a researcher of the brain, I have paid attention to one matter in many religious symbols. Namely, in cultures without modern medical equipment, a pinecone is a well-known symbol."

Without waiting for comments, he began to explain to the others, who waited for him to continue. "In addition to top of the Buddha's head in many pictures and statues, I have seen a pinecone form in the shape of Shiva's hair, too. There, like on those pictures." Olav pointed to the pictures on the wall.

The others listened with interest while tasting a most delicious meal, about which Ashmita told. "On the menu is dal baht. It's a spicy lentil soup over rice. In addition, we have curried vegetables, which are tarkari and momos, those pan-fried, stuffed dumplings, since mother loves them. Olav, very fascinating notions you have made. Please continue."

Olav'd just filled his mouth with rice, so Leevi was quicker. He swallowed and said, "I have seen in the Roman-Catholic Vatican a huge statue of a pinecone but also a small one in the wand of a pope."

Olav smirked. "In Egypt, a pinecone had been put in the wand of Osiris. Maybe the Sumerians had affected later cultures, since I'd seen a creature with a bird's head holding a pinecone."

Shilpa smiled and remembered one of her own trips. "I was once in Cambodia and saw the temple of Angkor Wat. Such marvelous towers, like giant pinecones. Why do you pay attention to pinecones, Olav?"

Olav spoke with enthusiasm. "Well, they first became familiar to me ever since I once gathered pinecones and sold them to a forest-care association that used them to produce new trees in different areas. But as a neuroscientist, I have learned a broader understanding of the words pine and cone. In the middle of the brain, the pineal gland reminds me of an eye that times the sleep-wake cycles. Sleep is, according to the pineal gland, the brother of death. The amount of DMT, or dimethyltryptamine, that is guided by the pineal gland increases while one sleeps or is near death."

Leevi tasted chili and mustard oil along with cinnamon and ginger. "This meal is so tasty, ladies! When it comes to the core of all religions and how people experience them, I think that you, Olav, just described much of that core. All religions are about being awake and sleep and understanding death." He wiped a drop of oil from his chin. "We all have similar tools in our bodies to experience and to reach an understanding of those. Religions from their ancient origins have tried to remind us about that. The core to me is humanity, an inbuilt oneness, which is common to all. People, whatever their religion, have an ability to develop as human beings. That is true religion in practice."

Shilpa looked at the others and drank some water from her glass. "Universal ethics is significant: do not harm others, really live like that, and do not make yourself a victim of your own weaknesses. No one is too weak to realize such a human skill. I guess that you, Olav, maybe have studied how meditation affects the brain, have you?"

Olav nodded. "The brain shows changes already after about two months of regular meditation. The brain is elastic. One can live even without one side of the brain, as one person did. The missing part was noticed only after his death.

Leevi contributed. "But reaching a peaceful, meditative state isn't very simple when there are many annoying matters around. To control negativity and anger can be difficult, as we know about human history." He was familiar with the history of the world.

Olav was prepared to respond. "You see, our brains have old and new parts. During our development, we needed aggression and fear to survive, so they still can have bigger power in our brains than do the kind and good interpretations of what we experience. We need conscious effort to keep positive interpretations as prevailing. That happens in the newer part of the brain."

"What kind of effort could be effective, in your opinion?" Leevi corrected his sitting position and straightened his back.

Shilpa commented. "I say that relaxing and concentrating seem to bring a human being most brightening effects. But I admit that concentration can sometimes be difficult, as can relaxing, too, in the kind of world and lifestyle people usually have."

Olav'd looked at them carefully while they were talking. "If we go back to our original question, have the religions failed in offering their best fruits for human beings? Or have the humans who've interpreted and used them lost the core point of humanity? What about science? It offers information, but is that used to bring good for all? Or, again, is it used as a tool to empty the globe and return what was taken as poisonous contaminant back to the vulnerable earth?"

Shilpa questioned him. "What if human beings weren't harmful but had fair and peaceful minds and actions based on humanity? Wouldn't those bring well-being and harmony and keep the earth livable?" She noticed that Rajan had left the room. She seemed to think hard and stopped speaking.

Olav tried to spark a conversation about religion and science. He missed Sophia as he remembered how they often wondered what the nexus was for the two topics. He said to Shilpa, "In many religions, people have the common belief that all was one in the beginning, and everything divided from that. The observations of science during our lifetimes have also found a common origin for all."

Shilpa looked at him with a slight interest in her eyes while another delicious momo found its way to her mouth.

Olav continued. "As time passed, religions have twisted from that origin because of the everyday lives and interactions of people. Most often, they changed into power games. Big ideas shrank into the manipulation of groups of people." He smiled and continued. "And what is more, science came along, like a religion itself. Did the observations of science about one origin and life as an interacting, living organism hinder the eagerness to destroy? Have you followed reports round the world? Anything can be demolished by human beings: land, flora, fauna, and other human beings in the name of getting richness from soil or good position for military strategy. Indeed, so many decision makers of states and multinational companies and people who support them have deaf ears, ignorant of respecting all life or others who are similar in their core as themselves."

Olav was still irritated by his own thoughts about the situation of the world. "I feel helpless. Science is often directed from a viewpoint of funding and a division of money. Many religions also are interpreted according to the interests of some groups. The core idea of science and religion about oneness and what it means often disappear, like people don't see the vital liquid under leaves or branches in a plant. How would we find a satisfying way to effect?"

"Very good to ask, answers will show up, I usually say to myself." Shilpa began to collect bowls and spoons. "Be patient. Maybe around the next corner is a best-suitable way to influence."

"Thank you so much for this nice meal and welcoming us here warmly." Leevi helped take some bowls to the kitchen.

Olav offered to help wash the dishes. He'd been up brought by parents who appreciated practicality, initiatives, and good manners in their only son. "Indeed, who would have believed that we would meet the family of Sophia's mother?"

Politely, his offer was turned down. His thoughts shifted toward the next day. "Now, are there buses going to Kathmandu today?"

Shilpa looked at him. "No, there are not. You can sleep in a spare room with Leevi. I'll show you." She stood up and took the men to a nice, small room with two beds and light, white linens, as well as a small table and a chair. "Now, you may be wondering how you will find our bathing and sanitary possibilities. Just follow me, please."

She took them outside to a building next to the house. "We have modern ways to utilize all we produce for recycling. Did you know that urine makes good fertilizer when mixed with magnesium? Bio waste will turn to earth again. The shower is here. A drill well gives water, and we heat it with two solar panels. Rajan has been very good at organizing all this for an inexpensive price."

Olav and Leevi admired the solutions. Leevi considered the sustainable use of the earth as a vitally important matter for future generations. "It is only a matter of time before recycling conquers the world. Even in northern Europe, it is handy to use solar power, since the summers are so bright."

They looked at the house under the half-moon light and admired its silhouette against the stars in silence.

Leevi was fascinated by the night sky. "This is a beautiful place you live in, Shilpa. Look, we can enjoy tonight's historical light coming from different stars. Some have just been born, and their light hasn't yet reached our sky. Other lights are from so far away that they haven't reached us yet, and some are giving their brightest fireworks in their deaths. The mystery play of life is open for us."

"Thank you, Leevi," Shilpa said. "And I do share your view. There is so much knowledge offered for us; puzzles and miracles are everywhere we set our eyes." She opened the door for them. "We shall continue tomorrow morning. I'll wake you up. Do you want to join a short morning practice for body and soul before breakfast?"

Leevi and Olav looked a bit surprised. "We do not want to disturb you," Olav said. "Just advise us on how to reach the place where Sophia was last seen."

Shilpa looked at them as if she were looking at small children with tenderness and affection. "You better get used to the idea that I will be your guide from now on. I believe I know where that dear, young woman is. The route there is best known by me. Anyway, we have a long way ahead. Sleep well!"

Inside their room, Olav sat on one of the soft beds and looked at Leevi. "My friend, I think that you should travel back home and wait there for news."

Leevi lay on the other bed with his hands crossed under his head. "And dear friend, do not try to escape during the night. You wouldn't know where to start your search for Sophia. You and I, we are stuck with Shilpa, and I have a feeling that she really knows even more than we do where Sophia is. I feel good about meeting Shilpa. I do not know much, but she mentioned that she lived her youth in times when her family was rich and she could study at least medicine and who knows what else in Kathmandu, Delhi, Melbourne, London, and New York. After some financial setbacks, and after her husband died in an earthquake, she surely has kept her spirit high. Her family has lost much, but she has taken good care of them and has helped many others with her skills."

Olav felt sleepy. "They have done a great job, and she is a strong woman and human being—a backbone for many. Sleep well. Hopefully, we shall find marks of Sophia tomorrow. By the way, did they tell to you about the family secret?"

"No," said Leevi. "I think that maybe not even all the family members know everything about it. Maybe Shilpa is the one who chooses who will know. Good night!"

CHAPTER FOUR

The morning was fresh in many ways. Dew on the grass and the spiderwebs were easily noticed. Sophia prepared breakfast by heating water for tea and steaming some momos made of beans and some other vegetables that she didn't recognize. She walked again down to the river to fill her bottles. She considered taking a cold bath. Only a couple of grazing tahrs were in sight, so she quickly took off her clothes and swam a circle in a rather strong current.

She felt energized and eager to begin climbing. She was glad that she'd practiced her muscles with different outdoor and indoor sports almost daily during the past few years. Her body was elastic and strong, and she felt like an ibex, fitted to this environment.

She jogged back to her tent to warm up her body again. She collected her stuff in her rucksack but decided to leave the tent down. She pushed it between two big stones.

While standing on a bare, bald rock in stillness, she heard a distant rumble. She felt alarmed and excited. Was the noise caused by rolling stones or something else?

She calmed herself. "It must be the waterfall."

The grass dried quickly, and ants had begun to walk across her left foot. She wiped the walkers to the ground and prepared herself to climb by breathing slowly and closing her eyes to pray and wish all the best for the attempt. She might have been silly to come here alone.

She began to climb, knowing that something special was going on in her life. Meeting Shilpa had opened to her a possibility to find a new viewpoint. It would be wonderful to share all this with Olav and Leevi, too.

The weak sound of down-rushing water had changed into a powerful noise. Coldness pervaded Sophia's hands as she sought her way upward with the help of tiny ledges.

Abruptly, she got a light, cold shower on the top of her head. The grip of her other hand loosened, and she hung with one hand, trying to keep her feet lightly touching the moving stones of the cliff. She noticed that she was very high above the ground.

No one would be able to find her for at least two days if she fell. A weak thought whispered in her mind that it would be easy to give up and let go.

She saw in her mind's eye Olav, Leevi, and Shilpa, who all trusted in her in their own ways. She knew that their good wishes followed her wherever she was. Suddenly, a feeling of endurance was growing in her.

One thought was above all: she wanted to survive. She saw a Himalayan tahr skillfully climbing far away from her. Its hooves had a rubber-like core, which allowed for gripping rocks, and keratin at the rim of its hooves increased durability for traversing rocky ground.

More power burst through Sophia's limbs as she watched and imagined herself being as skillful. She forced her shaky hand to find a small hole, and she hit one of her chocks there. She breathed heavily and tried to find new places for her limbs.

She gathered her strength and forced her muscles to move. Her other hand found a kind of root, while the second one found a spot for another chock, which helped her move ahead.

She decided to stick her rope there and rest. She let her feet be without tension against the slope and shook her hands.

She was alert not to rest in a too-relaxed way; the circulation of her legs could be disturbed if she wasn't careful. And help was far away.

She breathed deeply and let the peace of nature spread inside. The broad scenery over tops of evergreen pines, impressive mountains, and grazing tahrs that seemed so small from here gave her a feeling of tremendous freedom. That led her thoughts run to another discussion with Olav.

"Sophia, what's given you the biggest freedom as a human being so far?" They were in her lab, and Sophia'd just passed a plastic glass to him.

"It must have been the moment when I really understood how difficult it is, in fact, to define the word matter when its sublevels are scrutinized." She looked at him with her black eyes through her long lashes.

"What do you mean? How matter is connected with freedom?"

"Well, there is no universal definition for matter nowadays. We could study mass and the interaction that affects mass, or we could approach the issue by the definition that matter is constituted of atoms and molecules and, at finer levels, positive protons, neutral neutrons, and negative electrons. In fact, that is my favorite!" Sophia smiled and put her own plastic glass on the small table of her laboratory, where they shared a moment after last tasks. Olav had published an article, and Sophia had wanted to congratulate him right after she heard the news. They would soon go in different directions to spend the weekend.

She continued. "Olav, have you, in your research, thought what it could mean for a human being that there is an open question about all the energy in the universe? How much freedom there is in that state of no answer?"

Olav laughed. "We all are parts of this mystery and moving along with the whole universe. We spend most of our time taking care of everyday dilemmas, like what to eat for lunch or what other people think about us. Our thoughts and feelings are occupied by very practical matters. I have noticed that usually during exceptional experiences people can reach hints about that big, open question. Consciousness has its mystical way to work as well."

"I can speak only about matter. I find the whole issue funny, in a way, because of all observable energy, ordinary matter constitutes only four percent

when the rest is estimated to be in exotic forms of energy." It was Sophia's turn to laugh.

"Exotic?" Olav let the question hang in the air.

In her heart, Sophia had a little wish that Olav had said that if something were exotic, it was her eyes on a dark night showing a single, shiny star in each when the bright lamp of her laboratory reflected on them. She embarrassed herself by having such thoughts, and she continued quickly. "It means so-called dark matter, which holds twenty-three percent of the universe, and dark energy holds seventy-three percent. We do not exactly know what it is."

"Dark...Remind me why matter is called dark." Olav continued interviewing her.

Sophia lowered her voice and melodramatically emphasized this serious matter. "Dark matter doesn't emit or reflect enough electromagnetic radiation to be observed without help. Only gravitational effects reveal it. In fact, it is the force which holds galaxies in their shape."

"And if we want to go to the point that we travel all the time with the universe, dark energy is an antigravitational influence that is constantly accelerating the rate of expansion of the universe. It takes all apart. One day, there is a dark night sky when other stars except the sun are so far away."

Olav stretched his legs while sitting on the hard, wooden chair and rolled his shoulders. Sophia felt disappointed; she expected him to leave to his own lab, but he discussed further. "Those are very huge issues. What about the mystery of whole existence? I just wonder if it is the brain that makes us experience solid matter."

"How?" Sophia's thoughts still partly traveled like Voyager on the edge of the solar system and partly surrounded Olav.

Olav explained. "The brain works observational frequencies into the form of particles for an image, which resembles different forms of matter, just like our own bodies. Think about how despite this system of observation, everything is streaming like the living sea of consciousness. From that sea, one consciousness that is connected with everything picks up for her or him what she or he observes and lets it change to the 'reality' that we experience."

"That sounds mechanical." Sophia poured the last drops of her dry wine to her mouth. She took some water from her water bottle and offered it to Olav, too.

As he drank the water bottle empty, Sophia continued. "All this what we have is to my mind very fragile. Just think about the matter that is composed of the antiparticles of ordinary matter. If ordinary matter and antimatter meet, they annihilate each other; they might both convert to different particles with similar energy."

"Is that happening anywhere on the earth?" Olav wondered.

"We have that only in a very brief and evanescent form like lightning, cosmic rays, or radioactive decay."

Olav knotted his forehead. "That makes a mystery as to why we all carry on existing despite a possibility of vanishing."

Sophia enjoyed the memory of the conversation, as well as the breathtaking view in front of her eyes. She considered herself to be a tiny particle in the universe, which continued its mysterious being whether she observed it or not. Or did everything exist in order for human beings to observe and understand?

She hit her sharp, short prickles into the soft part of the cliff. She'd added them under her shoes with special decals. They were practical; she could take them away if necessary. She felt the cliff hard on her fingers.

After a long and sweaty while, she could peek to the next ledge, which was no broader than a bus. There were a lot of small stones that probably had rolled down from a faraway summit.

From this ledge, Sophia might finally get a good look at the roaring waterfall. She used both her hands to pull herself onto it and realized the ledge continued as a narrow path inside the waterfall.

She decided to take a break, for the air felt thinner. She planned to explore this slippery ledge and find out where it would lead her. She assumed that she would have to pass by the huge, noisy, wild, beautiful spectacle, and then she would reach the spot mentioned by Rajan. While thinking, she felt her eyelids droop heavily.

She felt dizzy. *This is a normal feeling, since the earth moves round its own axis at 1,670 kilometers per hour at the equator, but it travels round the sun even faster at 107,200 kilometers per hour. Yet that is nothing compared to the speed of the whole solar system, which moves round the center of the Milky Way at over 800,000 kilometers per hour, and it more than doubles the speed when it heads with its local group galaxies toward a so-called great attractor. At this very moment, they're all flying 2,200,000 kilometers per hour. I'm a passenger traveling in the space inside bigger and bigger vehicles of the universe. I must be part of a miracle.*

She remembered what she'd said to Olav.

"I constantly wonder how matter developed and began to scrutinize itself, wondering where its own limits are. Think of a form that stays as form. Despite the uninterrupted movement of what it consists of, it built societies and destroyed and invented something new for any era in question."

"But what originally causes movement?" Olav asked. "I have keenly studied consciousness. But I feel that it is more and more difficult to explain the essence of consciousness if one doesn't look in the direction of multidisciplinary research and especially toward subjective experiences."

Sophia agreed. "Indeed, the latter has been problematic for science. And when it comes to research, shouldn't a man have many qualifications that he could understand better and broader or even have any courage to believe what's been achieved in other sciences?"

Olav wondered. "That would be a huge work, but I at least confess that I have doubts if I can't make tests, observe, or experience. Should one human do research in many fields?"

That was the final whole sentence Sophia recalled until her thoughts broke. She had the blessed—or cursed—ability to relax after a heavy effort.

Sophia was dreaming. *She was having a conversation with a man whom she knew to be her near relative, even if she also was sure that she'd never met him, at least as an adult.*

A man of Sophia's age and with dark hair and eyes screamed. "But I have a mass! Here my body is under microscopic scrutiny. Can you see? Now I exhibit wave-particle duality: waves…particles. Oh, the interacting energy of elementary components of my body give this handsome body most of its mass. And with a mass, millions of neutrinos go through.

"Sophia, here we are in subtle levels, protons and neutrons, but look closer. In fact, we are in the level where quarks and the force fields bind them together. And electrons in deeper level are leptons." The man sang, and his voice came from far away as the distance between them increased. Then his voice came again, nearer. "Nevertheless, there still is the mass."

Sophia felt very light. She explained to the man. "A single resting particle, photon, has no mass. It's light. Its mass is just zero."

The dream continued. Sophia observed an empty space filled with energy and vibrating particles, which her theoretical mind called fibers. This field was full of movement.

Sophia wondered if consciousness could be a similar field.

Leevi's face appeared next to her and spoke. "On the border of consciousness, I can choose a channel. It is like a TV broadcast that I can watch when I choose the right channel. I am part of all this!" Leevi laughed.

Sophia considered in her dream how she could hear Leevi's mind and the mind of a man so familiar to her, whom she should know.

As immediate answer, one of her own textbooks opened to the page about the hologram theory. The page shouted to her. "Once, the smallest parts of matter had been one. After spreading around, they still affect each other. See the big picture. This is the origin of the universe; this is the present!"

Then Sophia saw how all was in one spot, and then a giant explosion forced it all to separate.

Leevi's voice sang. "Still, everything has knowledge about everything else. Just choose the right channel in you!"

Sophia was coming back awake as her dream continued its wishful conclusion. *Shilpa was walking forward and in deep thought. "So, ultimately, knowledge about everything is relatively transparent and available to anyone who can raise their energy high enough?"*

Leevi stepped right behind her. "Yes. The point is that people are not interested or devoted enough to raise their energies. If they were, that would evidently be taught at home and at school. I could imagine that somewhere in the future this richness will be a natural part of all human beings. Just imagine how much it will change interaction and living conditions of human beings and our relation to all that exists."

Sophia soon understood that it had all been a dream and that she must have taken a nap, for a sudden scratch made her flinch. She smelled wet fur near her. She turned her head slowly and saw a small, smoky-gray snow leopard with yellowish underparts. Its light-green eyes looked right into her eyes until Sophia turned her head a bit.

Sophia speculated the cat was still young. What a beautiful animal, she thought as the creature tried to open her food bags. She tried to scare him away by throwing small stones and making noises.

Sophia hoped that the snow leopard's big mother wouldn't appear and attack. As the young animal disappeared inside the waterfall, black rosettes shined on its fur. Sophia was amazed.

She threw her rucksack on her back and pushed her climbing tools behind a big stone. She left some lock rings dangling from her waist.

She hurried after the small snow leopard and tried to mind her steps on the slippery ledge. The rumbling waterfall that she was approaching was almost like a living being.

CHAPTER FIVE

Shilpa woke Olav and Leevi with some knocks on the door of their room. Both men were in deep sleep because of the time difference between continents and all the new information and experiences they processed yesterday. "Good morning!" Shilpa said. "Anyone eager to do some morning exercises for body and soul?"

Leevi rushed up to Olav. "Let's go, my friend. And for your information, you spoke aloud during the night."

"Did I? Please do not tell if it was something embarrassing." Olav was afraid that he'd spoken about warm feelings toward Sophia. That would have been too early for her foster father's ears, and even Sophia didn't know.

"Where shall we have the silent moment?" Olav asked Shilpa.

Outside, they were greeted by Ashmita and her older children and went to sit facing the rising sun. Shilpa led them to a purifying breath at first. They did some energizing asanas and finished the short session with Shilpa's guide to meditate on the eternal oneness of all beings.

Leevi felt peaceful. Olav began to relax despite all his worries about Sophia.

After the exercises, Shilpa changed from her green sari and blue top to practical, gray trousers and a jacket. She had a brown cap covering her black hair, which she had tied into a ponytail. Only a few shiny streaks of gray showed. She then led Leevi and Olav to an old truck, where she laughed. "You looked very surprised to see this old pickup. As Rajan said, it is well kept. He managed to buy it among many worse used cars. Jump in, please! We can all sit here in front. I have put some food stuff in the back. Throw your rucksacks there, too, please!"

They all sat in silence, looking at rebuilt villages that they passed by. They waved to some people, who returned their greeting. From time to time, Shilpa stopped the truck to give rides to some men, women, and children, who rode in the back.

The route Shilpa'd chosen didn't go through big towns. Nevertheless, when they passed by fields and villages, they realized that there weren't many places without inhabitants. They admired the villagers; so many had rebuilt their lives with trust and hard work after the earthquakes.

"Leevi, please tell me about your life," Shilpa said. "How did you end up adopting a child from abroad?" She held the steering wheel tightly as the truck went down one hill on a narrow road and a lorry passed by it, almost touching the truck's side.

Leevi smiled at his own memories. "Where to begin…There was a time when I was a young farmer with cows, lambs, chickens, and fields, too, like so many here in the countryside. Cold conditions were challenging to the harvest, but selling eggs, wool, milk, and sometimes stocks balanced the economy of my family in long winter seasons. One day, a summer trainer of agriculture, named Olga, came to practice at our farm. She had dark, curly hair and dark-brown eyes."

Shilpa was interested to hear about her sister's foster mother. "What kind of person was she?"

"She was a practical, down-to-earth person. I'd say that she felt a strong connection with the earth." Leevi became enthusiastic. "She put her hand to the warm soil and smelled the fragrances that different seasons and their winds brought along. She loved the colors of nature, from the greenness of summer to the red, orange, and yellow of autumn. She painted now and then in the silent winter days, when the sun was down and a starry sky provided light. The pureness of snow in its blue light and frost was magical to her. Besides light, Olga liked the dimness and its secrets, which emanated a gentle hope for everything."

Shilpa laughed. "Oh, dear me. I'd like to experience those seasons and winter, too, as you describe them. Not to mention how lovely it would have been to know Olga."

Leevi continued with warm voice. "She was a personality, indeed, a soul mate evidently to me, maybe because we understood and saw each other's innermost beings. But simultaneously, I had a feeling that we would never reach each other's depths. I can say that we celebrated our love as a gift. We were such a wonderful team, especially in taking care of common matters, the biggest of which were children. We could have only one due to a complication of a first child birth, so we welcomed a baby through adoption."

Shilpa nodded. "And so Sophia's mother, Silja, came to the family. Our parents named her Poonam."

Olav had felt tired, but now he was alert. "According to brain research, affection is the best and longest-lasting part of so-called love when passion passes by."

Leevi addressed him. "Olav, you might not be a big friend of romance. I can say that we had twenty-five amazing years, during which we could share tears of joy and sadness. It was sharing that made us whole and kept us together. I know that some people who've lived differently spoke that we were wandering in the middle, lacking adventures, that we were middle class and modest, like daisies rather than roses. But Shilpa—may I use your first name?" Leevi noticed that they hadn't agreed on using first names. Shilpa nodded, so he continued. "Isn't it so that the color white contains all the colors, so they would all be in the petals of a daisy, too?"

Shilpa nodded. "I heard from Sophia a tragedy befell Silja."

"Yes, there were in fact two bad incidents." Leevi blinked several times, as if something had got in them and needed to be rinsed away.

"Oh? What do you mean by two?" Shilpa accelerated because a hill was in front of them. They were high above a village, where people did their daily chores among their cattle and fields. Their car approached a curve.

Leevi felt an empty feeling in his belly with the sudden lurch downhill, but it was also because of his sad memories. The silent beauty of white-topped mountains ahead encouraged him to continue his story.

"Well, Olga and my two daughters were in the car. Silja insisted that they hurry, and so they did. Suddenly, a reindeer jumped in their way. Because of black ice, the road was slippery, and my wife lost the control of the car. They crashed against trees. I won't go into details, but as a result, my wife and daughter Eva died. Silja was the only one left alive."

"That must have been awful," said Olav with empathy. He felt worried being a passenger while Shilpa drove. He always preferred to be the driver and have control instead of being a passive passenger.

Leevi continued. "Silja always blamed herself about it. I was kind of paralyzed and didn't want to see life anymore. Cataracts even grew over my eyes."

"How did you cope with that?" Olav's foot made movements like breaking and giving gas as he followed how Shilpa drove.

"I didn´t cope well at all and only after some years I lost Silja, too. Her and her husband's other child, Sophia, was left to live with me. That was a turning point."

"How did you lose Silja?" Olav hadn't ever heard that part of the story.

"She felt guilty, and even if she got a family of her own, the atmosphere in it wasn't best for her. All the time her husband criticized her and was encouraging her to think that she wasn't enough. You see, Silja, a punishing master of herself, had attracted to her a king of mocking and criticism. Finally she committed suicide. Her husband wanted to raise only the boy and left Sophia to me. And that was my savior, even thought it was tragic to separate the twins."

"And where is the other child, now an adult?" Olav was curious.

"Leo is his name. His father took him abroad without telling where they were or keeping in contact with us. I would've loved to know Leo."

Suddenly, a yak stood in front of their truck. Shilpa braked strongly. The animal was huge. His thick fur covered him all over.

"What a marvelous animal!" Olav shouted and took a photo on his mobile phone. He then put his phone away inside his shirt pocket and resumed questioning Leevi. "How was Sophia as a child?"

"She woke me up from my winter sleep. She was the sun against my night. She gave morning light back to my heart and eyes as well." Leevi waxed poetic, his eyes shining with affection. "I took my responsibility very seriously and thought her time with me was a gift from the universe." He continued with a lighter voice. "I was astonished about her curiosity. No insects or plants were insignificant to her. She was enthusiastic about everything. For me, it meant that I could once again see life more openly, without preconceptions or a broad selection of associations colored by experiences. She had endless questions."

Olav smiled. "Oh, she still has! A magnificent quality in a scientist."

"She even asked about things that were not exciting in her time, such as 'Why isn't there a swing outside anymore?' That was a tricky one, since the trees that held the swing had been sawed down a long time before Sophia was born. I tried to find out more, but you know how children are. She'd already forgotten her question and did forward and backward rolls in dry hay. I still remember how a distant thunder made that summer afternoon cooler." Leevi reminisced and smiled silently at his memories.

"How did you have time to take care of her with all that farming?" Shilpa's practical mind tried to get the whole picture of the situation.

"When my daughters were small, I was tasked with many chores, but I really could be devoted to Sophia, since I'd given up the cattle and retired early due to my wife's death and my own condition after that."

"Did all these happenings affect your concept of life and death?" Shilpa blinked when lightning flashed through the sky and the day went grayer. Soon, grey clouds would fill the whole sky. "It has always been for me difficult to understand why Christianity does not have reincarnation."

Leevi's voice was quiet. "People who lived in certain times had a meeting and decided about it long ago. It's been written in stone ever since."

Olav wanted to share his research knowledge. "But many people have experienced something other than what a social agreement says."

"Please continue, Leevi," Shilpa said.

"I'd had certain experiences, but I didn't remember my childhood incidents when I was surrounded by despair. The world's religions and cultures always have appealed to me. For instance, a Tibetan death book said that a certain kind of life takes place in the state between lives. It takes a while until the stream of life invites one back to a body and surroundings, which match with the energy one had when one's life on earth ended. But as I understand it, the journey all the way to the ultimate beginning, the source of origin, would be longer. If one could meld with it, life would be so pure that it would be lighter than a feather, as the Egyptians had so aptly described it. But even after that, one can return to the world to help others." Leevi thought about the humble spiritual teachers throughout time.

"There are texts that say the development of a human soul takes many cyclical phases. Some of the phases are as long as 25,920 years." Shilpa thought of the huge time perspectives they were dealing with.

"Oh," said Olav. "The very same period had been known also by Plato, and that's why it is also called a Platonic year. In astronomy, a precession is a change caused by gravity in an object that is rotating. In this case, it describes a constant change in the direction of the earth's rotating axis. That cycle is 25,920. After this, it comes back to the position from which it started to change."

"So, as being a human soul, a journey inside oneself can be the longest of all trips." Leevi said. "After the two incidents concerning my wife and daughters, I literally prayed and cried to find any reason for the incidents, some sense and truth as to why they had to die, as well as any excuse for me to continue living. I wanted to choose the life. I sought for truth and found many answers. This searching is a task of life that we all have. There are no ready answers, but we must think, ask, and listen in silence and be alert to life situations about answers that life will give."

"What do you mean?" Olav asked.

"Some answers can already be part of our experiences, but we can forget them if we are too deeply in sorrow. I remembered again my childhood experience of being outside my own body after I almost drowned."

"Can you describe it?" Olav was interested to know if the description would be similar to the ones he'd found out through research.

"Abruptly, as a child, I glided through a tunnel toward a light and saw my short lifespan as a film in my head. I looked at my little body when the adults tried to revive it. A light was ahead. It was inviting, but it asked me to return to my body. So, I did. I was pulled back to my spluttering and coughing body when the adults managed to revive me. I told them that I saw and heard them all, even though my body was on the ground, eyes closed. The adults laughed, except my grandfather. He winked and said, 'Better that you talk about these matters only with me. Many people do not understand, and they are afraid.' But my grandfather knew, because he'd experienced a war and had seen a lot of death, as well as revivals. He knew that the ones who came back from the border of death and life might have experienced something extraordinary. He also knew a few cases when a person who'd lost a limb had felt and seen his body whole again during a near-death experience." Leevi's face was heavy in concentration. "Later, when Sophia told me that she often played in a place while sleeping where all is light, I had an insight of a lighter level of existence."

"So you had experienced life after death in a near-death situation and much later heard from Sophia about a lighter life possible to experience during sleep?" Olav tried to confirm that he'd heard right and took a bit of a banana he'd taken from his snack bag.

"I understood it gradually when pondering experiences. One can't die, not even if one wants to, like Silja. And what is that lighter place? I tried to understand for Sophia, even if for her it was something natural till the age of seven."

"Why do you think that it ended at that age?" Shilpa opened the window a bit more to let the wind play on her face. Single water drop landed on her cheek.

"A soul has to adapt and get used to living in a human body and the circumstances and challenges of each life. That is why past lives aren't usually remembered. Remember that she also concentrated in everyday life mainly through her senses, but during nights while sleeping she could enjoy the lighter level of existence." Leevi was silent for a while. "If the inclinations are toward developing oneself, the energies still need to be opened and kept purified in each life. The world and one's own body give constant challenges."

"You mean every time when one is born to live in a human body?" Shilpa confirmed.

"Yes, but no doubt if the sensitiveness are already high when one is born and experiences are memorized, as in Sophia's case, the yearning to search for knowledge and develop oneself can be even stronger."

"Well," said Olav. "I spoke earlier about DMT. A human being has the natural inbuilt equipment or ingredients—whatever you want to call it—to reach such experiences. But when it comes to near death, there have been some studies. To me, the most impressive was a case where a woman who'd been blind all her life saw colors when she was outside her body. She was revived, and she could tell about that, even after she became blind again when she was back in her body."

It had rained for a while during their discussion. The truck stopped and didn't move forward. "It looks like you need to push," Shilpa said calmly.

The men pushed. Their muscles ached, and they sweat a lot, getting mud all over them. But it was worth all the trouble; after many trials, they got the truck out of the mud. Some monkeys stared at them from the trees nearby, watching the entertaining show.

"This mud," Leevi said. "It reminds me of heavy thoughts in which one can get stuck, and willpower is needed to be free again."

"Sure," said Olav. "As I've said, human brains are so structured that negative thoughts get more attention, just because it was a way to stay alive during human development. But it takes willpower and decision making to maintain good viewpoints, too. I agree."

Shilpa joined the conversation. "I'd say it's possible to choose any object for concentration. Thoughts can always be lifted toward higher levels, and similar thoughts will then attract and join them. That happens to negative thoughts as well. One can surely get similar thought levels accompanying those, too." She felt satisfied behind the wheel when the truck was free. "But closer to the silence of mind, one leaves all the thoughts and listens. I'd say that is surrendering to a higher level in oneself. But jump in the truck, now, please. We have still quite a long way!"

They drove on and admired the valley below. After the rain, thousands of small water streams were glittering in the colors of the rainbow. The travelers held their tongues and enjoyed the view. Nearby on the branches of a tree, they saw reddish brown fur moving. Almost simultaneously, they said, "It's a red panda!"

"Hey, it has little cute cubs," Shilpa said. "How very beautiful! Do you have something like this where you live?"

"Some predators, like bears, wolves, lynxes, and foxes, for sure, and they all are very protective of their little ones," said Leevi. "But they usually do not want to face with people but hide and avoid meeting them." He was satisfied to have the opportunity to familiarize himself with some local animals.

"Isn't it amazing how animals take care of their little ones?" Olav asked. "They keep them near till they learn to cope for themselves. How many people don't care for their own offspring?" He remembered how cruel humans could be. "Many are ready to follow their desires but not so ready to carry the responsibility. For some people, children are commodities."

Leevi nodded. "Indeed, humans have developed many ways to be cruel toward the weak and vulnerable. But do not forget that anyone can make a change and become a protector and helper at any time. It just needs to be chosen as an attitude of life."

Olav pondered that even charisma could be used to promote evil. "Just how often have you seen the power of mesmerism and mass suggestion when people want to spread hatred and cruelty among other people?"

"All the misuse of others and indifference can grow to big systems when people do not want to think for themselves and find out the truth but believe blindly and act accordingly. Also, myriad drugs have been used to encourage killing and inhuman behavior." Leevi had heard many stories about drugs used in war.

CHAPTER SIX

The noise of the water was almost too much. Sophia felt as if it would go through her ears as huge, constant, painful sound waves. Now the rays of light that morning brought along were reflecting countless rainbows gleaming on the water's surface. They made an unreal atmosphere in the middle of the transparent fog and coolness of the down-rushing water.

Sophia stayed awhile to decide if she wanted to keep her clothes dry. Hypothermia was not an option she liked to choose, but a cold shower wouldn't do any harm. Calmly, she took her clothes off and put them inside the rucksack, which she covered with her body by bending her back. Then she hurried her steps.

Sophia blinked because of the water drops, and at first she couldn't see anything when she stepped into the corridor inside a cliff. She entered under the waterfall and into the corner of the huge hole.

She felt heavy, ice-cold water hitting on her back and head. It made her laugh. The fresh coldness and the tapping on her back reminded her of big hands giving a strong massage.

It was rather dark and slippery inside the cave. She went farther, holding her rucksack like a precious baby. When the distance to the waterfall got bigger, the light began to diminish.

It was time to put her clothes on and take a torch to get some light.

She smiled to herself. What a way to step in the secret route of her family. She felt as if she'd come to a natural holy place. Her body was cleaned and awake. She wished that her mind was also open and ready for whatever she would face.

She felt happy and satisfied after a successful climbing. Her record wasn't exactly heroic, but she felt good despite the water dripping down her legs in a most uncomfortable manner. She enjoyed this excitement and challenge, even on such a small scale. She continued walking in the dim light, and suddenly she was in an even broader space.

When Sophia's eyes got used to the lamplight, she saw the walls of this space better. There were small stones but also a kind of stone formation, the surface of which shone from the humidity. As she let the light dance on the walls, she noticed signs: a square, a circle, concentric circles, and a spiral that ended the line.

She wondered when the signs had been written on the hard surface of this cliff. Maybe Shilpa's ancestors had made them.

She was thrilled. She could not concentrate properly on her thoughts. She had to be alert for observations. She went on deeper inside the cave. Just then, she could see a big, black hole on her right side.

Some excrement of a small animal was on the ground. She walked forward and felt a weak shiver from the cold. The humidity penetrated her clothes, but there was something else. She stopped and listened, but all she could hear was the wild noise of the waterfall.

She got the sense that someone was scrutinizing her. She supposed the young snow leopard waited nearby in ambush, and Sophia would be her quarry.

"I'm a bit too tough for you," Sophia murmured aloud and continued walking, shining her torch before and after her as she went.

CHAPTER SEVEN

"Oh, look! A monkey came to travel with us!" Olav laughed.

"A rhesus macaque." Shilpa stopped the truck. She didn't want this passenger to lose her social contacts with her own group.

Leevi wondered aloud. "What a long journey the universe made to develop a body to a human soul. Why do so many not respect the possibility of being born in a human body?"

"That is a universal question," Shilpa said. "Many people would rather become slaves of manipulation, money, and a leadership of a charismatic dictator. Think how different the world would be if people would help each other like brothers and sisters, help the weaker and vulnerable, and give to them encouragement and shelter."

"Thought waves, as well as spoken and written words, are a powerful weapon in the right hands," Leevi said. "One can lift people from the swamp of anger, fear, and addiction."

Shilpa stepped out of the truck and offered apples from the food bag to the monkey and to the men, too. "We have to come back to the world as long as we learn to know ourselves and reach our full potential as universal beings and part of the whole universe."

"Maybe," said Olav. "What do you think, Shilpa? What are our chances of finding Sophia?"

Leevi bit into his apple. "I'm very worried about that issue, too. But we must maintain good thoughts about this matter."

"Cheer up, both of you! She is a strong woman with wonderful spirit." Shilpa began to collect branches. "Let's make a fire so that we can warm up our meal: a spicy vegetable soup will be on the menu! Hopefully, you love garlic and chili. Let's have a fireplace between those stones. I have to tell about my worries concerning my son Rajan."

"I can light the fire," said Leevi. "What about Rajan? I have noticed that we may need to be very careful what we think and say about other people, since the quality of our thoughts of them add to that kind of energy in their aura. And they tend to affect their reactions to us."

"I am not sure," said Shilpa. "But I can't totally trust that Rajan has been honest with me concerning Sophia. He is a good son, but he can sometimes feel jealous and undermine himself, which can lead to harm in others. But I want to trust that he won't go too far with that."

"I want to keep the hope up," said Leevi. "But having said so, I admit one important matter that affects human relations. When we were born here, we carried different loads of karma with us. That old load and even sometimes new load from this life comes active in situations that we have to live through. Anyway, we are not powerless. We can actively add the amount of higher-level thoughts, not certain subject or content, but higher level, whatever that means in a culture one is born into. In a so-called atheistic culture, it can mean oneness of mankind." Leevi managed to get a small fire, which hungrily ate some dry branches they'd found.

Olav was alarmed and anxious. "If there are some worries concerning Rajan's behavior toward Sophia, we better hurry. He did disappear yesterday, didn't he?"

"I am not seriously worried, but I have questions about him in my mind." Shilpa wanted to take back her words. "We have time to eat, and we need all energy to complete our journey. Please calm down, Olav."

Olav wanted to take his mind off from worrying too much and turned to Leevi. "You mean that as we all have different thoughts, we add amounts of certain thoughts among people, even when we have some distance between us. But with effort, we could change ourselves by thinking more and more higher-level thoughts." Olav sat on a stone near the fire.

"Changing a habit of thinking is a process. We usually tend to return to our old ways of thinking, and that is reinforced by thoughts coming from people who think alike." Leevi had experienced that several times himself. "For example, if we have low-level thoughts about ourselves, we feel sorry about ourselves and powerless. And if people would think about us like that, it would generate pity among groups. Finally, we would be in a vicious cycle, or even a jail. Our surroundings would support that energy to stay around us."

Leevi continued. "And then it happens that we hear or read an inspirational thought and lift ourselves up to joy. It's a crucial moment if we hold that powerful thought despite what our surroundings would think of us."

"Is that a changing point?" Olav was putting more branches on the fire.

"If we hold long enough with that, we won't go back to our old ways of thinking, and we begin to change the way others think around us. The secret is that all of us have had at least the smallest spot of light inside ourselves ever since we were born in a human body. We can be magicians who change ourselves to new kinds of persons."

Shilpa decided to confess. "I have to admit that I still find some weaknesses in myself, like not trusting my son, and then I sometimes expect the worst of him. Maybe that weakness prevents me from promoting the final steps in my meditation toward a stage where a meditative state of mind is prolonged. Constant worrying, even if it happens in the background of thoughts, eats good energy."

"Yes, and irritation is so usual toward people we live with." Leevi considered family life as good practice to evolve as a human being.

"Why do you think that's so?" Shilpa asked as much aloud as to herself.

"The closer we come to ourselves, the more difficult it is to comprehend the truth. Our own colored specs are the most difficult to notice. They are, after all, on our own nose and build on our own precious thoughts and feelings." Leevi took a water bottle.

Olav pondered and massaged his neck. "I think that the idea of perfection is rather dangerous. For some, it's difficult to admit good sides in themselves because they know they're not perfect; for others, it's difficult to admit having any bad sides because they expect themselves to be perfect as such. People near us tend to reflect what kind of specs we have."

"I agree," said Leevi. "Who better reflects us either as opposition or as similarity than the ones near us? But with the truthfulness comes compassion; a true humanity includes development. Do we really want to close our loved ones or ourselves in cages of low self-esteem or too much pride to see clearly broader points of view?" Leevi had found some interesting white stones and rolled them on his palm.

Olav was now stretching his body on the grass. "One matter is still unclear to me. Who was waiting for me with a gun?" He thought that now was as good a moment as ever to find out about that confusing detail of his trip.

Shilpa shook her head. "I do not know, but I have a hunch that Hira or Rajan had accidently mentioned your arrival to a person who didn't like the idea. This is probably nothing, but when we drove along the trip, I thought I saw a certain motorcycle follow us. But now that we have stopped, it should have reached us. So, chances are good that we are by ourselves."

"You didn't tell me about any gunmen," said Leevi to Olav. "Not that I would be too worried, but why on the earth would they be interested in you?"

Olav jumped up into a standing pose. "What's the secret, Shilpa, that you haven't told yet? Could it be a reason to use violence?"

"No, it is nothing material that anyone could benefit from. I'll tell you about it just a bit later. I would say that the gunmen were on the wrong tracks and have by now understood their mistake."

CHAPTER EIGHT

Rajan looked out the window of the helicopter without paying attention to the scenery. He remembered how he'd given a long talk to the two men who didn't manage to bring Olav to him. Instead, he'd been surprised in the house of his mother and sister.

When Rajan realized that two men from northern Europe had arrived to look for Sophia, he was forced to make new plans.

He'd given one man a new task to follow a certain pickup truck at a safe distance just to find out where it ended up and then inform him.

His own work he considered harder. Still, he thanked his god of good luck that he'd found a shortcut that had appeared in the mountain route after the earthquakes. He had to use it carefully, for it happened to be a dangerous place. Yet it was the best way to let Leo in the tunnels of a certain cave.

A doubt that Sophia had succeeded in her climbing ate at Rajan's peace. He had to confirm that Sophia and Leo wouldn't meet each other. He hadn't yet decided what to do with Shilpa and the two men.

Anyway, what Leo did was between Rajan and Leo. Nobody else's business was to intervene in that.

It'd been a silly risk for him to believe that Sophia wouldn't climb or find her way to another route too near the place where Leo did his job.

"What a mess!" Rajan ended his memories and thoughts when he arrived at the place where he could land with the help of a rope ladder inside a hole, which was very near the place where Leo was taking his samples. Rajan had previously brought supplies here for Leo as well.

CHAPTER NINE

"Hey, there are some antelope-like animals!" Leevi opened the widow to see better.

"Those are Himalayan serows." Shilpa knew the fauna in the area. "Did you know that there have been fossils of serow-like animals that date back seven millions years ago?"

"No," said Olav. "I didn't know, but I studied that the Himalayas are an old sea bottom that continues rising." He was fascinated by the earth almost as much as he was fascinated about the brain.

"Sure, look at these fossilized ammonites." Shilpa showed a stone where the form was clear. "I have found them on the slopes of the Himalayas."

"You mean coiled marine cephalopods—hard evidence that this area was a sea in ancient times." Olav was enthusiastic. "History tells amazing stories."

They drove awhile in silence, looking excitedly at bushes and trees. Maybe more animals would show up.

"What about karmas of nations?" Shilpa was curious to know the others' thoughts.

"What do you mean?" Olav scratched his head.

"There has been colonialism; after independence, civil wars; and after those, wars between nations; and again wars because of risen emotions or inequality in society concerning ethnicity and religion. Neighbors have confronted neighbors. It's as if people can't help but clear relations outside and inside countries with the help of violence." Shilpa concentrated her sight on the road and saw from the side mirror that a motorcycle was following at a distance behind them. She thought that she might have seen that before, too.

Leevi was sitting in a relaxed position. "When a nation chooses a person to lead it, the person may prove to become a dictator who gathers like-minded people who gain special benefits and appeal to lower energies in a human and demand others to be similar. Then, in that kind of regime, measures are taken to maintain power by all means. Low energy grows with lies, fear, and corruption." He stretched his legs, wondering why Shilpa insisted on driving all the time. What a woman she was. She helped her whole family and neighbors. Leevi admired and respected her.

He continued in a peaceful voice. "We do live in many places in time when spiritually low-energy people can rise in power and cause suffering for good, peaceful people. They even harm people's bodies in order to rule their thoughts and feelings. That leaves much to clear for the whole nation to become truthful for generations to come."

"I would say that all cleaning of energies begins with individuals," Shilpa said. "In many countries, the situation is like in medieval times: people are persecuted and tortured because of their thoughts and kind actions." She checked now and then to see if the motorcycle was still behind them. It was.

Olav was tired, but the conversation triggered him. "It's amazing how some ruling powers believe that a change toward broader consciousness is dangerous. They'd rather feed despair and hopelessness to keep their own regime."

"Between individuals, the reaction is so often the same." Leevi often pondered how difficult it was for leaders of nations and single human beings to be honest and put themselves in others' positions.

"What is the solution?" Olav enjoyed the company of these two persons.

"We people would win all that with compassion, similar as one can feel toward a distant mother and child. People's innermost beings are not different." Shilpa felt empathy toward all mankind, and she didn't comprehend the relation between power struggle and inhuman behavior. How could anyone treat others badly?

Leevi nodded. "Just think if supporting higher thoughts would begin from childhood instead of people learning to undermine and put down or develop superiority toward people in less fortunate situations. How beautiful the people's auras would be, how they would flourish in their full potential and affect their surroundings." Leevi had seen beautiful auras, big and radiating. Most auras were filled with worries and fears. What a blessing that love and affection toward children and family members was also very frequent. Unselfish love was seen, but so were selfishness, jealousy, and envy. The more unselfishness was an aura, the more impressive and effecting were the energies.

"That is a great theory." Olav's mind turned to Sophia and how he missed her. "I would be interested to know how Sophia, our matter specialist, would see that."

CHAPTER TEN

In front of Sophia, something glittered and radiated in the weak light. She turned her torch on. Despite its small size, it was effective and gave light to a narrow, stony corridor. The walls were a bit shiny because they were covered in white quartz refined by nature. Some spots even had rainbow-like reflections because of the moisture.

After the corridor was more open space. Its floor glittered with quartz in some places. When Sophia took a closer look, she noticed that water was streaming under the floor of this cave.

Sophia went deeper inside and wondered. There was a new corridor with several other corridors that opened like black holes in front of her. She wondered where to step in and which one appealed to her. She closed her eyes and tried to feel how to choose. She opened her eyes again and noticed that she'd moved toward one of them unintentionally. She decided to go forward. All in all, she had to choose seven times.

Sophia stepped slowly into the seventh narrow tunnel, minding her head because of a low ceiling. There were numerous cavities on the wall, which were filled with transparent groups of stones. Sophia's skin on the top of her head tingled, and her palms felt like they'd touched thin cloth. She put her hand on a stone, scrutinizing it in the lamplight. *This could be quartz, very clean.* She knew that it was made of oxygen and silicon. Her brain told her the details: The quartz structure was usually presented as four adjacent tetrahedral-type units. Quartz could be described as a network of interconnected tetrahedrals. There were channels in it that ran through the crystal molecule.

Simultaneously with her flash of memories, she felt as if a stream of electricity were moving in her spine. Her mind was clear.

In her mind flashed an image about a spiral galaxy.

She now knew matters that she couldn't have ascertained by herself. The meaning of the symbols on the walls of the cave where she was earlier had simply appeared like a self-evident fact through her crystal-clear mind.

Matter like a human body served a developing consciousness until consciousness became a conscious part of the universe.

She could hear Grandpa's voice explaining that Grandmother Olga used to wonder how matter circled and offered a human being this material manifestation of the universe to use as a body for one's lifetime.

She felt humble. Indescribable serenity filled her, as if her eternal home had been this small space, as well as everything outside it: white, snow-capped mountains; waterfalls; rocks; stones; every plant and animal; energy; and space. All was part of her, and she was part of everything.

CHAPTER ELEVEN

Leevi was still in his thoughts, looking at the now-blue sky above them. Clouds were quickly sailing away. "What do you think the reality really is?"

Olav scratched his hand. "I would say that the structure of a human being's brain as an observation system has limits, but it also has abilities that can reveal more than five senses. All this affects what we think of being a reality."

"In my mind, what we can observe depends on what is our inner development as a human being." Shilpa was almost sure that a motorcycle had followed them. Had Rajan sent it?

Leevi had been glad to see how impressive and clean Shilpa's energies seemed to be, even if she had some worries. "I also see limitations. My viewpoint is built on the basis of how a person thinks and feels, which builds an aura round a person. So, there can be a jail or bubble built with different desires, anger, and fear, through which everything is seen a bit twisted or colored by prevailing feelings and thoughts."

"That sounds rather right that a person has certain repeated ways to react." Olav knew that he, for example, always wanted to analyze all that was his habit.

Leevi continued. "The importance to develop oneself can begin especially with noticing what the thoughts mostly circle about. That controls the inner reality, and one needs to overcome it so that one's own will is in control instead of certain compulsive thoughts or feelings. One can search for higher thoughts and feelings and add them consciously." Leevi was also satisfied with the high intelligence in Olav's aura. That would help Olav, if he wouldn't become imprisoned by it. There was a border where the analytical mind could go on the journey to self-awareness.

"You have very visual way to approach this matter, Leevi," Olav said. "Do you think that the whole human system changes when the higher level is reached?" Olav was interested in Leevi's way to see, despite having a hard time imagining what Leevi in fact saw.

"Indeed, that is what I think, for example, if a person manages to control anger and replace it with empathy. It changes the colors, hues, and forms of thought and feelings in the aura. Furthermore, it changes what one attracts and what one spreads around." Leevi had seen that kind of change. He'd witnessed how peace of mind was reached little by little.

Olav thought a moment. "So it could be that what we observe and pay attention to depends on our level of inner development. Interaction is maybe the right word." He turned to Shilpa. "You spoke very generally, Shilpa. What is the highest point of development for a human being, in your opinion?"

"You may know that on the way toward perfection or full blossoming of human potential, a human being can reach many skills that broaden observations and actions, as well as knowledge to a new level. Still, to reach the final goal, the truth, all forms will be passed by, and pure consciousness means becoming one with the ultimate truth."

Leevi wondered. "In human history, there have been rare people so pure minded that they haven't had any negative thoughts, feelings, or energy, if you prefer that word."

"But the rare, pure ones have been able to change the people around them," Shilpa said. "In the heat of the moment, anyone can make a change and influence the course of matters." Shilpa knew people who'd affected their surroundings, whose presence calmed others.

"That kind of mind control as a permanent skill means that there is no tantrum, either," Leevi said. "When we are children, we just learn to recognize our feelings and moods. Children need protection to safely train the use of their feelings, thoughts, and energies. Usually, they get protection from adults." Leevi remembered how he'd been like a sheltering energy to Sophia when she was small and vulnerable.

Shilpa took the soup that she had made at the house the day before and added it to the kettle, which Leevi moved over the fire.

"But who protects an adult?" Shilpa asked. "I say they must learn to protect themselves. They need to learn to know their energies profoundly. Otherwise, they can be easily manipulated and led by the energies they have gathered most so far." Shilpa spoke on behalf of education, especially self-development among women and men. Both were primarily developing human beings.

Leevi decided to share a visual description of a process when energies moved. "Indeed, you've spoken about situations when a nasty, heavy energy tries to penetrate someone's aura. When it cannot find a matching vibration, it finally returns back to a sender whose vibration is matching. But just think what a big role fear and a negative attitude have, since they welcome energy that is alike and ensure that the worst can be experienced. Spiritually, we have the possibility to be untouchable, but it's not easy to leave fears and negativity behind. That can take a lifetime or more.

"Finely is the body built for a human being to experience what is necessary to advance in humanity. Matter meets the demands of a developing soul." Leevi took a spoonful of soup to his mouth. "Delicious once again! You make my day, Shilpa!"

"What about artificial awakening of brain areas with drugs?" Olav was well aware of addictions and their effect on the brain. He'd seen much research.

Leevi smiled. "Do they leave a good, lasting, and uplifting feeling and a clear mind and understanding? No, I say. They make a person a slave, not free. What is more, if you ask questions while meditating, you can find all the answers concerning the universe, life, and death. You will go beyond forms toward the ultimate truth." He spoke with passion.

"What would be a good way to reach that kind of wisdom and truth nowadays?" Olav wanted to challenge himself.

"Different types of human beings are suited different ways," Shilpa said. "Some need to be active and spread around their kindness and help others; they might have inner knowledge as a born gift. Others need to think about traditions and religions of the world, its history and present. Then there are ways to reach oneness and silence first as an inner experience." Shilpa had studied in many countries and learned about many religions and cultures.

"What ways do you have in mind?" Olav couldn't wait to hear.

"One tradition is called Nyingma. In it, a limitless experience of presence is reached by maintaining feelings of bliss and infinitude for longer and longer periods. Some people find it easy to concentrate and listen, first maybe with the help of a mantra, or a sound that releases the mind with its vibration. Then one can also meditate so that the total silence of the mind is prolonged little by little. It results with patience to limitlessness and oneness." Shilpa poured more steaming soup for herself. Through the steam, distant tops of mountains appeared to be in a blurred photo.

Olav narrowed his eyes and spoke with a tickle in his throat. "You've really put some garlic in here, not to mention the chili, but it's only a good matter. Thank you, Shilpa." Olav then recalled previous researches. "But to mention about the use of some skills in life…I know that during the Cold War, some individuals exhibited clairvoyance for finding out the secret hideouts and projects of other countries, including the development of new weapons."

Leevi roiled the hot soup in his bowl with a big spoon. "Special skills can be of great help to people. Just think of Edgar Cayce. He'd given analyses of health and advice to people for years. He didn't have any formal education in medicine, but he had right diagnoses when he went into trances while seeking answers."

"Helping others is always right, as long as no deceit is present," Olav said. "I always speak for everyday heroic actions. We all live and die, but who has the courage to care and help or change oneself?" Olav had pondered a lot about what made evolution so difficult. "You know the biggest hindrance on anyone's path is oneself. It's exciting that others can in fact help by having good, higher thoughts. When are people most responsive for thoughts that are intentionally sent to them?" He took a water bottle offered by Shilpa.

"I think that people are more responsive to others' thoughts while sleeping or in a relaxed state," said Leevi. "For instance, one can intentionally send healing or higher thoughts. That can be connected to a practice that stretches consciousness. One can send higher thoughts near or broadly and see his or her own consciousness in different sizes, whether as broad as the world or tiny."

"Hmm," Olav said as he finished his last spoonful of soup. "Lower parts of the brain work then free from the control of the upper part of the brain. Also,

I would say that in meditation, the experiences of omnipresence and oneness are caused by the fact that the activities of the left side of the brain, as well as the parietal lobe, are temporarily suppressed, and more space is given to other parts of the brain."

"Now we need to put all in the car and continue." Shilpa stood up and began to collect bowls.

In the pickup truck, they sat side by side. Shilpa drove, even though Olav and Leevi both offered to drive in turn.

"You can drive when we come back," Shilpa said and changed the subject. "Have you had special dreams lately?"

"I did have a dream last night," Olav said. "My first childhood home was like the sun. I was naked like a newborn, only a kind of yellow flame was my cover. What it could mean?"

Leevi answered. "Olav, it represents a pure you as you were born. And that light of your first home reminds me once again about Sophia, who said she played in a light place in her dreams when she was no older than seven." Leevi had stored that knowledge deeply in his mind. He understood that Sophia had spoken what she really had experienced.

"Thank you, Leevi. That sounds fantastic! What do you think, Shilpa?"

"Was there a sound of a thunderstorm?" she asked.

"Now that you mention it, I remember that there was lightning and a low, powerful sound. The flames round my body—was it a memory of a past life as a burnt witch?" He laughed with nervousness.

Shilpa's eyes sparkled with gladness. "As I understand it, I'd say that you awakened yourself, and your subconsciousness gave the image that your supraconsciousness knew! You are more than a form-changing body; you are a spirit!"

Leevi remembered what he heard when he and Olav had shared a room at Shilpa's. "You said aloud while sleeping 'valo,' which means 'light.' That is also symbol of your own name as in a mirror, the side that is not manifested in lower-level frequencies."

"I understand a changing body, like from a baby to an elderly man," Olav said. "Or do you mean taking a different kind body after death when born again? And do you mean that I can know in consciousness the part that is not manifested?" He began to phantom drive with his feet again, using invisible break and gas pedals while Shilpa drove.

"As a human being, you have a so-called causal body," Leevi said. "You develop it with your own choices. Then in the end, after death, you have in it information on what kind of body and circumstances you need to face. What is the state of your development as a human being? It can take a long time until suitable conditions and parents for a certain soul appear. If the nonmanifested part of you would join physically with you, then you would disappear, be annihilated." Leevi looked at them.

"That makes sense," Olav said. "Sophia has spoken about matter and antimatter in her physical terminology of cause, but now I'm beginning to understand what it could really mean for existence of the world. Human beings have consciousness that can experience invisible matter and antimatter. This is huge." Olav whispered with astonishment.

Leevi laughed. "Isn't it? In our society, not many generations ago, people were told that they were just bad, useless, and without willpower or expectations. This was more popular than believing they were as perfect as their creator. I think that a human has all possible equipment in the body to reach full potential and be one with a cosmic, universal truth that includes all. The more open society becomes and offers possibilities to develop oneself, the more people will search for truth."

"This all is very interesting," Shilpa said. "I think that we all need to smelt the information that we shared. Soon we have to leave our truck." She prepared them for the walk.

The sun began to set behind the mountains, giving them orange and amazing violet colors. The breathtaking view silenced the group. Shadows of pines grew bigger, and the evening star was already seen in the sky. Next to a deep rock, Shilpa drove the truck between trees. The group covered the muddy vehicle with a green-black, plastic tarp that Shilpa had in the back.

"Ready or not, now we walk and then go inside." Shilpa took her rucksack from Leevi.

"Inside where?" Olav was ready but wanted more details.

CHAPTER TWELVE

Leo drilled the rock wall. *Taking samples is hard work*, he thought. He recalled what Rajan had told him.

"I know a place where there's treasure. I can show it to you if you pay enough."

Leo had taken the bait. He was a hunter of treasures and opportunities to do business. He'd counted in his mind what he could ask from some businessmen if he would find palladium or other interesting stuff. He could sell any jewels he found.

He needed money for his own studies about artificial nanoparticles that could be planted to humans. He could earn a countless fortune from that, no matter who his customers were.

Indeed, even so-called peaceful states produced and sold weapons that were used almost randomly and ended up in the hands of warped-minded persons. Why wouldn't he take his share of money available? Most important was to move the money, make business, and have free markets. He had big plans. "I'll pay half now and the rest when I find something," he'd told Rajan.

Rajan had taken him here through tunnels and labyrinths. Fortunately, the helicopter flight to a certain hole had saved much time, and Rajan had kept him well equipped through that place. Rajan had showed to him a cave that had something interesting on the walls.

Leo had wanted to work in peace, so Rajan had gone to deal with what he called an urgent family matter. But he'd promised to come back after two days to help him with equipment and samples, as well as to make a final decision if they would continue their business.

Leo put down the drill to rest his hands when he heard footsteps approaching.

After her wonderful experience Sophia decided to go back to the waterfall and go down to wait for Rajan, but she began to hear a drilling noise from the tunnel. She was astonished and wanted to find out what was happening.

She reached the noise's source and saw the man from her dream, the man she should have known. "What is this? Who are you?" she asked.

At the same moment when Leo noticed her from the corner of his eye, Sophia felt someone placing a soft cloth over her face. Rajan had arrived from the other direction and subdued her with a rag soaked in chloroform.

CHAPTER THIRTEEN

Shilpa smiled and turned her back. She walked inside a bush, and Leevi and Olav followed. Shilpa knew it was better to travel through bushes and not through open spaces, even if it would have been easier. Big rocks blocked their way, and the bushes were especially dense. Shilpa took her rucksack from her back and began to crawl between two rocks, pushing her rucksack in front of her.

Olav couldn't help mumbling. "What on earth is she doing?" But he still followed her. After what felt like an hour, Leevi breathed humid air and made space for Olav. At first they couldn't see Shilpa. But then she switched her lamp on.

"That was the easy part," she whispered. "Just some humbleness and crawling like a baby, and we now can walk again! Her eyes shined in the artificial light.

"Why do you whisper?" Olav's voice was normal.

"For one main reason, this entrance and route are rarely used, and the mountain is kind of living. It grows all the time due to continental plates. Earthquakes are not strangers. Here can be moving stones that are waiting to fall. Our voices are waves that can cause movement. This can be dangerous from now on, but we have already spoken about death and what can be after, so I expect that you are willing to take this risk to find Sophia, as I am, too.”

Leevi smiled. “Sure we are. Thank you for helping us.”

Olav agreed. “No two questions about that. We are here because of it.”

Shilpa smiled. “Follow me, and do not go by yourself to any other tunnel or cave out of curiosity. It is easy to get lost here. Also, move carefully; slippery rocks cover the way.” She turned the lamplight to show the way ahead.

Olav and Leevi used their own lamps to see where they put their steps. Their clothes began to suck in the cool humidity, and they could see water drops all over the narrow tunnel in which they walked single file. After banging his forehead twice on the low ceiling, Olav needed to mind his head almost all the time, keeping it slightly down.

“Maybe I didn’t tell you before, but I must confess that I have slight claustrophobia,” he said.

Shilpa calmed him. “Do not worry. This route follows the natural wrinkles of these mountains, and there will be plenty of sky to be seen and fresh breezes to be felt from many natural holes and tunnels that curve following the slope.”

Olav kept his eyes on the narrow lamplight that his small headlamp offered. He had to concentrate on his breathing and decided to force his thoughts away from the tightness of the place. He knew that his anxiety made him speak almost incessantly, which helped with his phobia.

"Look, what a stalagmite!" he said aloud when his lamplight reached a huge structure of growing stone pillars.

Shilpa whispered. "Listen, please." They all heard a rambling noise.

"What is that?" Leevi's voice was very quiet.

"Some parts of the mountain are more open to its other parts through natural channels. The noise can be a waterfall inside or outside the mountain." Shilpa decided that it was water and not stones that made the noise.

Olav wanted to be sure and listen longer. "Wait. As a neuroscientist, I should be able to understand that when I do anything with concentration, I can bring my brain to a certain state. Then a kind of turbulence in the temporal lobe and in the lower parts of the brain can open me to a knowledge that normally is hidden behind the practical knowledge that is so necessary for actions."

The others looked at him, pale, and Leevi waited for stones to start falling. Yet Olav continued. "And that hidden knowledge can open up for any human being who doesn't have too many 'filters' switched on." He ended his speech in a quieter voice.

Shilpa turned toward Olav. "You see, Olav, a human being can in many ways be connected with the energy around him or her. Knowledge is available and in that sense transparent."

Leevi participated in the discussion but began to walk ahead, as he decided that was the best option. "And at the same time, one is connected with the basic energy in oneself. All is vibration. When a human makes his or her mind and senses silent and turns his or her attention inside, then it's possible to get a better connection with the energy that vibrates around."

Shilpa passed by Leevi and took the lead. "Or a human being can increase one's own vibration while noticing beauty, thinking higher thoughts with music and so on. There is harmony and beauty even in the smallest matters in nature, like in the petals of a tiny flower or reflections of a water drop, but also in big matters like the openness of the sky."

"Indeed," Leevi said. "Think how purposeful all the measures and distances are exactly perfect for the life to manifest and maintain existence for this globe and around it. That is some crown of harmony on a macro level." Leevi followed Shilpa, making sure that Olav's light was behind him. He smiled to himself. "Some people raise their vibration by singing or saying prayers for others. Good, benevolent thoughts lift vibrations. As we spoke earlier, one can even intentionally send them to others on a broader or smaller scale. Then after a while, when one nurses this kind of inner treasure, nasty feelings and thoughts do not hold easily, or they stay in one's mind for shorter and shorter periods."

"I have a question," said Olav. "Is there any example where a human being has reached higher vibrations?"

Leevi thought what would be near Olav's background knowledge. He knew that Olav was raised in a Christian family. "For example, if you are familiar with the world's religions, you know concerning Christianity that in the Old Testament Moses went to the mountains alone. After returning, he had to hide his face because so much energy came through his eyes."

Shilpa wanted to bring the phenomenon to a broader context. "I also know that some mystics can raise their energy levels so high that they can sense, hear, or see knowledge from the ageless source that is reachable everywhere."

"Sophia seems to walk inside this mountain, too," Shilpa said as she stopped to wait for the others.

"Why do you think so?" asked Leevi.

Before Shilpa answered, Olav spoke. "In my soul's eyes, I got a flash of Sophia walking inside the cave deeper inside the mountain. She seemed to smile to herself, and a flame-like light covered her. It was stronger around her head."

"You two seem to have become more sensitive," Leevi said. He couldn't be happier for them and for Sophia. "All these special experiences can be hints that maybe we are getting nearer to our goal."

"Or we influence on each other in the way that sensitivity rises," Shilpa said.

CHAPTER FOURTEEN

When Sophia awakened, she felt weak and hopeless at first. But she got her spirit up again, despite the darkness all around her. Encouraging thoughts streamed to her. Again, she felt the presence of Olav, Leevi, and Shilpa.

Her character had always been optimistic. It was her basic attitude toward life, and it had carried her so far. It helped her float in a sea of life when the world was filled with bad news, worries, threats, and fears.

Now she happened to be in a relaxing state, half sleepy, and her optimistic thoughts grew. *I'll cope as always. I'll find solutions. I'll get help. If someone tries to harm me, the situation will turn toward the best outcome for me.* She whispered to herself, feeling the moisture of the stones through her clothes.

A narrow light came near. Then Rajan, the son of Shilpa, stepped into the small space where her hands were chained to the rock wall. Lamp light revealed that her lock rings, had been used for this nasty purpose. "I am truly sorry, Sophia, cousin, that this happened to you," he said. "I am fully aware how much my mother respects you, but she should have remembered that I am her son, worth several of women like you!" His voice began to go higher as he let his anger and frustration burst out. "I wouldn't believe that you could climb up. If I knew you were able to, I would've never let you see that the route really was there."

Sophia looked at him in the dim light. She noticed that she could see his aura. In a flash of thought, she pondered how visible light was only a little amount of all the electromagnetic radiation. Each star sent a constant, bright spectrum that had lines. The basic elements of the star in question could be identified in those lines, which represented its elements. Now Sophia thought she could read the basic feeling and thought level of Rajan in the radiation around him.

She had wished this ability before and knew the meanings of colors related to levels of feelings and thoughts, for her grandpa had explained them. But it was different to have this tool in use. It was like a built-in spectrograph for identifying basic feelings and thoughts of a human being, not the content but the level of them.

But until now she had not been able to observe them herself. She was glad about this new viewpoint and thought it to be a side effect of her experience in the quartz cave.

She saw how Rajan's anger grew in his aura. Red flashes surrounded him on the black surface. "Calm down, Rajan." The red spots of irritation stayed with a red flash of long-held anger. Sophia tried to locate his higher thoughts, even though that could be too difficult when the power of emotion had imprisoned him. "It's all right. I won't tell this to anyone. Just let me go. I know that you are a good person who prefers to protect the women of the family."

"Whatever," Rajan said. "I have to go and check some matters elsewhere. I leave these fruits for you. I advise you not to disturb Leo Stone. He prefers to mind his own business. You must wait here till he is ready. Then we decide your fate." He put some bananas near her. Sophia felt like a chained pet—not a very pleasant feeling. Without more words, Rajan left her in the darkness.

"Where are you going?" Sophia shouted after him. No one answered.

CHAPTER FIFTEEN

They'd stopped again. This time, they were between huge rocks in a corridor that continued toward a narrow space with the open night sky. It must have rained, for there was water on the bottom that ran over their feet. They looked at each other and tried to breathe calmly.

Shilpa's voice was calm. "Now, we have to squeeze ourselves, and I am afraid that we have to unpack our stuff partly to get the rucksacks to the other side of these two rock walls."

Leevi, the slimmest of them, went first. "Please give me the rucksacks one by one, and I'll pull them to this side."

Leevi felt a cool breeze and enjoyed the fresh air, although his feet were wet and he began to feel cold. "Just try not to breathe too deeply when you are between the rocks. I'll pull you in here when I get a grip."

Olav felt nervous and tried again to think of something else. "How do you overcome low-energy situations and go back to balance or cope with them so that they won't affect you too much?" He stepped between the stones as deeply as he could.

"Indeed, the jail or possibilities for oneself are so much built by oneself," said Leevi as he reached to have a good grip of Olav's hand. He continued explaining. "One can often learn a lot from bottoms and highs. One learns to compare light and darkness, sadness and joy."

"Do you mean the tool of attitude?" asked Shilpa, pushing Olav on the shoulder with all her power. "When one decides to choose an open attitude, life changes toward possibilities and limitlessness. Everything good can be possible."

"Do you mean an ability to see broadly?" Olav tried to breathe slightly and shallowly. "Depths, darkness without any light, endless anxieties, black moods, and fears dissolve, forming the hill on which one can get his or her high enough to see more broadly. I experienced that after my divorce."

"Mind control saved me," said Leevi. He pulled with aching arms on Olav's left hand. Nothing happened.

"How did you carry it out?" Olav thought that he was permanently stuck. He was sorry for both Shilpa and Leevi. Now they would have to go in different directions, and Leevi would surely get lost.

CHAPTER SIXTEEN

Sophia—a slim, energetic woman—was now swinging on the borderline of consciousness and unconsciousness. It would have been so easy to give up and let the unconsciousness take her along, but Sophia's will was well practiced to follow her own dictates, thanks to countless exercises and versatile psychic activities. Usually, life in the world was, to her, filled with cosmic humor. She understood abstract, complicated concepts; to her, the world was often like a scientific box in the universe where mysteries and paradoxes shook hands.

Even if she was captured now, her mind would travel in freedom. Despite the floppiness of her body, she was well aware of her environment, a small space.

Sophia's mind was becoming clearer. Her thoughts ran at high speed, and she remembered her motto: *There's no use in being sad about matters, since there's so little observable matter anyway in the universe and only a tiny bit in a human.* In fact, if the equipment that had been invented so far revealed the ultimate truth, all reality was, on the level of subtle energy, mostly nonmaterial. But what kept it all together in shape and movement so a single atom didn't dissolve immediately into smaller parts? Whose will? Whose power? Whose TV program?

Recently, Sophia had returned to these particular issues with Olav. A few researchers whom Sophia knew, like Olav, had connected the sciences. And when it came to Sophia, she was still like a child filled with questions.

Sophia had carefully studied how the known physical forces—gravity and electromagnetism, as well as weak and strong interaction in the core of an atom—had a field that affected the matter around them. She'd raised a question with a number of scientists, especially Olav: Could consciousness also be a force that held a shape for observation? Olav had said, "In extrasensory experiences and out-of-body experiences, a person has a better connection with his or her whole awareness, which seems to include the universe. In this way, a single consciousness can be interacting with the whole universe."

Sophia felt the irresistible need to laugh. She imagined how Leevi would join their conversation with his own viewpoint. He would surely have stated that now Western science shook hands with mystics, yogis, and others who ended up with this answer after their subjective experiences.

She remembered vividly that Olav had started to become carried away by optimism and had swung in his chair. "Yes, and think most of mankind is not at war, despite feelings of irritation and different opinions. During the lifespan of a person, his or her observation system repeats from the beginning a certain 'reality,' and so is building an image of the world shared in so many ways by the majority of mankind."

A light blinded Sophia and interrupted her thoughts. Leo stood in front of her. "So, Rajan told me that you are Sophia Harmony. Do you know who am I?"

Sophia knew that she should know the answer, but she shook her head.

Leo continued. "You were born fifteen minutes after me—"

"Leo! Glad to meet you!" Sophia said in a mumble. She tried to read his aura and saw a lot of yellow intelligence with reddish orange pride, brown selfishness, and irritation with red spots. "Let me free. Rajan has lost his mind—temporarily, I hope—and did this." She had hope in her voice.

"I can't. Maybe Rajan believes whatever you made up for him. But to me, you have to tell me honestly. Why are you really here? Are you taking samples for some technology factory? What have you found?"

Sophia looked at his irritated, suspicious face and felt helpless to explain. "Now, you know that even if I happened to work for a section of environment and human development in an international collaboration association, this has been my personal journey. If you saw my rucksack, there is nothing I could use for taking samples. So, just let me go, and I will not spread word of your business here. I give you my promise."

Leo shied. "How stupid do you think I am? You've left them to any tunnel you used before you came here. You are in chains for your own good. I don't want to waste time to run after you. It's better to retain control of any insecure piece of a puzzle. That's one of my mottos."

CHAPTER SEVENTEEN

Leevi kept talking and pulling Olav's hand. "I understood consciously how important it is to keep the mind stable, clear, and clean from doubts. It is no use to let thoughts run away to routes where they would get sticky and dirty. It would be so difficult to get rid of that. Some careless thoughts might cause one to fall; if it happens too much, a person can be stuck between depression and anxiety or in repeated hurricanes of anger. It is vital to keep on trusting. Doubts would attract fog and negative streams with strong suction. Those would blur the vision, take anyone's feet off the ground, and thus remove a basic trust. If I may suggest, could Shilpa give a good kick on the side of your bottom?"

"Yes, can I?" asked Shilpa, trying to see the humorous side of the situation. "That sounds like a very common-sense suggestion."

She pressed her both hands on the cold rock walls on her sides to get some support and kicked without waiting for an answer.

"What?" Olav couldn't say more because he fell with high speed to the other side. He would have fallen in the cold water of the narrow corridor if Leevi hadn't been holding his hand. He'd felt a sharp pain on his shoulder during the process.

"Do you have a special place where you meditate these matters?" Shilpa's voice came from their side as she pushed herself behind them.

"Interesting that you ask," Leevi said. "Because of the trees around it, I call my small hut a serpent-spruce cottage. It is in the wilderness, with no roads to reach it. It is the place where my deepest, best silent moments have taken place. I can say that the serpent power in me has been like in the surrounding serpent spruces there. Once it found a way up, it surely reached out, no matter how curvy it had been." Leevi laughed, as if he understood his own hindrances and stages on the steps of developing himself.

He looked at Olav. "Are you all right, Olav?" He saw that his friend had a painful expression.

"This is nothing, just a sharp pain on my upper arm, but it'll surely pass by." Olav shook his hands. "Thank you both. That was a clever idea!"

"It was a pleasure." Shilpa laughed and set her rucksack again on her back.

"You would have done the same to me, Olav," Leevi said. "Shilpa, in my meditation place, a strong power similar to a roaming thunderstorm once traveled from my perineum along my spine. The stream went through my head and carried my consciousness via different levels until it spread limitlessly."

Shilpa was curious. "Olav, did you notice the description of roaming thunder in this connection?"

"What do you mean?" Olav asked.

Shilpa explained. "The expression of a powerful energy source opens inside a human, and it begins to travel up in subtle energy center while consciousness broadens."

Olav concentrated on the openness of the indigo sky. They all knew that they couldn't stay in one place for a long time.

Shilpa hurried them to continue. "There can be more rain. If it comes with power, this narrow spot can be filled in a few moments. I'd rather save my swimming desires to later needs." She didn't reveal what was ahead.

They walked slowly. Olav shook his hands from time to time, which diverted his attention from his phobia. They arrived at a large pond, which glittered in their lamplights in yellow, brown, and black, reflecting off the walls of the cave.

"I can't believe it," Olav said with amazement.

"It seems that we'll have a nice, fresh, evening bath," said Leevi as he sat on the narrow edge over the pond. He could see his own face in the lamplight reflecting back. Single water drops from the cliff ceiling caused concentric ripples on the pond's surface.

"We can keep our clothes mostly dry if we take some off and tie them in our rucksacks." Shilpa began to open her rucksack. "Olav, could you go first. We'll throw all rucksacks over to you. What do you say?"

"Sounds fine!" Olav said. He and Leevi simultaneously began to remove their shirts and trousers.

"So does it take long to be able to maintain broader consciousness?" Olav began his questions while paddling in the water. The others showed light for him, even though he had a headlamp. The lights smelt together and gave a feeling of safety inside their group. Olav heard the sound of manual charging of one of the lamps that Leevi held.

"How clever of you, Leevi, to have that kind of torch!" Olav's attention was focused on the coldness that ached his feet. He was grateful for the extra light. When he swam, his hands broke his moving reflection on the surface of the pond.

Shilpa spoke to calm them all. "Usually a feeling of bliss lasts until a negative thought and feeling stops it. But little by little, after recharging oneself again and again, the periods of serenity will be prolonged."

"So, there are states of meditation?" Olav asked with a shivering voice. The water was icy.

Shilpa put a big scarf around her in the safety of darkness and put her trousers and shirt in her rucksack. Then she walked to the cold water and began to swim. "After the joy and bliss have been successfully maintained, there will be a state in which a human being feels joy because of creation. Due to increasing consciousness, human beings consciously contribute to creation. After that, while still in a body, a human being can reach a state in which he or she observes and recognizes the divine simultaneously inside and outside himself or herself without a difference."

Olav pulled Shilpa up from the cold, silky water.

Leevi directed the lamplight for Shilpa. He checked that the others were up and began to throw the rucksacks. He managed well except for one sack, which fell on the hard ground. They all could hear something break. "Whoops, that must have been someone's lamp," Leevi said. "Can you check?"

While the others were digging in their rucksacks, Leevi estimated the distance according Olav's headlamp, which was on the other side but not really shining toward him. "I find the growing consciousness in one's human body a wonderful fate. Just think about it, so immense the universe, and its parts will be one."

He stepped in the water and spoke slowly. "Broadening consciousness takes the fear of death away. I was such a doubting person that I needed two different personal experiences until I was convinced. As I told you earlier, one was in the serpent-spruce cottage, and one was in childhood when I almost died. I know now that I'll keep my consciousness through death, too, and just have a lighter form. Ah! My foot is stuck between some stones."

He disappeared from their sight. Olav gave his headlamp to Shilpa and jumped in the water. It was dark under the surface, but Olav happened to touch Leevi's foot and found the stones that were trapping it. He used all his muscle power to move the stones. He noticed that his left arm was not as well as it used to be, but his right arm worked well. He was worried that Leevi couldn't get air, so he lifted Leevi's head above the water.

Leevi's eyes met Shilpa's worried ones, and he spit some water from his mouth so he could yell. "All's well, Shilpa." After that, his head went back under the water again.

Some stones began to drop around them. Shilpa moved near the humid wall but continued showing the light with Olav's headlamp.

Olav popped his head above the water, inhaled deeply, and disappeared again. Small stones dropped after him. Shilpa stood alone by the pond and couldn't believe that she'd lost her travel companions.

CHAPTER EIGHTEEN

Sophia saw a narrow light approaching the place where she was chained. Leo entered again in front of her. "Sophia, are you ready to tell your big brother now what you searched for in the cave?"

Sophia let her eyes scrutinize Leo's slim cheeks and eyes, which looked as if he had a constant fever burning in his mind. *Maybe he does*, she thought, with warm sympathy in her heart. "If you hadn't given me something to blur my mind, I could understand better what you're after," she said. "Isn't your expertise in chemistry and nanotechnology?"

"You're an eager user of the Internet!" Leo shouted. "I know a thing or two about you as well! Still, you don't know really anything about me. I happen to be a multitalented man. Here, I have found some interesting minerals for any company's use. I'll use the money I get for better purposes. You should know that affecting people's minds gives true power to them who have most of the control. You or your association do not know anything so far. People need strong control and discipline, especially women. I am developing something—"

Sophia interrupted quickly; if Leo revealed his secrets, she would never be set free. "Leo, I am well aware that you were brought up by your strict father, and our mother died far too early, but that is not a reason to burden other people."

"Don't speak rubbish! I grew up with realism. Weak people need supervision and guidance, and they are useful for their superiors, who can at least take some advantage of the hard work for taking care of the masses. The well-being spreads out to the masses, too. They have more food, houses, things, and entertainment to fill their lives with. If you ask them, that is what they want."

Sophia was puzzled about how to speak with Leo. "I think that all may have a yearning in their hearts to learn more about themselves and the world. Entertainment sure helps people understand their feelings. And sure, well-being is much about filling basic needs. Still, we wouldn't need to enslave each other to reach that."

"You do not understand. Just answer my questions. What did you search for in the cave, and what do you hide?" Leo was fed up with Sophia. He found her to be quite boring. Luckily, he could live with his father. Leo wondered why he'd bothered searching for information about Sophia. *There's no logic in that*, he thought. He was dissatisfied.

"Have you met our aunt Shilpa?" Sophia asked, her tongue in the middle of her mouth.

Leo looked amazed. "No, I don't know anything about mother's relatives, since her adoption papers had been missing, as my father knew."

"Well, I met her, and she recommended this route. So, this is just my personal journey to respect the ancestors on our mother's side. Her mother was from

India, and her father was from Nepal. Because of unfortunate coincidences, they happened to be in a bus accident. Our mother survived and, due to a misunderstanding, was defined as an orphan who was given up for adoption. Shilpa happened to be visiting her grandparents while the rest of the family was on the bus."

"What are you trying to explain? What misunderstanding?" Leo was becoming impatient.

"During the accident, the baby—our mother—flew out the window when the bus lost control and rolled over down the road. Everyone inside was dead. No one could find the baby. But she'd landed on soft hay and leaves, and a Sherpa who was passing by later found her. She was unharmed, and he took her home to his sister, who took her to an orphanage run by some missionaries. They organized adoptions to families. It all began to clear up for me when I accidently met that Sherpa on one of my climbing trips. He recognized me from the birthmark on my neck. I dug through old news and found out about the accident and the missing baby of a young couple."

Leo looked at Sophia's brown spot on her neck with amazement. "And now you claim that you were here only to pay respect to an old family story."

"There is an old legend that's passed from generation to generation. Grandfathers and grandmothers have continued to tell it to their children."

"And so what? The world is full of legends." Leo was despising this story.

"Sure, but you should hear this, since you may be part of it as one possible actor."

Leo laughed. "Be serious!"

"There is a prophecy that there will be born a girl and a boy who will face the truth about human beings on earth while inside this very mountain to fulfill beauty and goodness. They have already in this life opened a door to eternity, but only one of them will understand what they face and live accordingly." Sophia's hands were hurting because she couldn't move them properly. Why had Rajan and Leo captured her? She was harmless. Why had she been curious enough to check the noise of the drill? But she knew why.

Leo was part of the legend. Yet, he hadn't experienced the magic of the place or understood when she'd tried to explain the possibility to him.

Leo put in front of her a little bowl filled with some soup. "Here, eat. I have serious work to do." He turned his back, and the light from his headlamp disappeared.

Sophia was hungry, so she decided to taste the contents of the bowl. Slowly, she moved her hands and touched the side of it. She lifted it to her lips and drank half of the strongly spiced liquid. The taste was somehow odd, so she poured the rest to the side.

She began to feel sleepy and soon dreamed again. *When the power that uplifts all vibrations is released, people's ability to observe will jump to such high dimensions that confidence in humanity's miraculous existence won't be hidden from anyone. Then everyone could be free from fear and worries and get up from the swamp of ignorance and anxiety to flourish in a stream of versatile possibilities. Like dandelions in asphalt holes, people would live in relation to the old concepts of the world and life and lift their heads toward a bigger light.* Through the dream, she felt coldness increasing in her limbs. Some small stones rolled down over her. Was the mountain waking up?

CHAPTER NINETEEN

Two heads appeared again from the water, and the men swam to Shilpa, bruised and cut. Olav had a big red spot on his cheek, and Leevi had a gash on his head.

"What happened?" Shilpa whispered. She was worried that sound waves would wake the loose stones again.

'I don't know exactly," Leevi said. "But when I splashed in the water, like I usually do when I swim, one foot went between some stones and didn't come out without Olav's help." Leevi held his right foot in the lamplight.

Shilpa studied it. "We're lucky. I see only bruises and minor cuts. I shall use some disinfectant to clean that wound on your head. I have some wound glue with me in the rucksack."

They clothed in silence. Shirts and trousers were not totally wet but humid and muddy. The group filled their water bottles from the pond.

Leevi's teeth were chattering, and he exercised his limbs to get himself warm again. He continued his comments as if nothing had happened to him. "But I must say that maintaining consciousness might not happen to everyone immediately. It must depend on what kind of condition a person is in at the moment of death. Maybe a rest would be good at first, after the challenges of life."

"I'm not sure anymore if we're going straight or round or simply lost in these endless tunnels," Olav said. "I can't wait till we have trains here like the ones going through and up the Swiss Alps, or perhaps we'll establish a huge research center to study the secrets of the universe, like they study dark matter in Italy." Olav joked but was half serious.

He'd given his headlamp to Shilpa, who walked in front of him. Olav tried to see where to set his foot according to Leevi's lamplight, which danced right behind him. Olav's own shadow was the worst hindrance for him to see properly.

"All is well, Olav," Leevi whispered. "We can trust Shilpa. I believe what my instincts say. They trust our direction to be right. As for a railway line here, I don't know. The mountain is rising up more than the erosion is wearing it down, compared to the Swiss Alps. Also, earthquakes are more common here. Furthermore parts of these mountains go slightly down when other parts go up. Maybe there will be solutions to build in the presence of instability in the future."

Olav's phobia had risen again, and he needed to shift his attention. "There have been no signs of human beings wandering here, only humid rocks and stones. In a strange way, the curving, dark tunnels remind me of the structure of the brain. If we compare our situation to the brain, we could be somewhere in the middle, maybe near the pineal gland, when outside on the slopes of mountain is the surface where most of thinking activity happens."

They felt a blow of fresh air from somewhere above. The space around them became bigger, and the ceiling rose higher. The smell of some plants increased. Leevi and Olav blinked.

Green junipers grew under a big hole, which was far above.

"The greenness is partly pale, but plants are living here, and lichen is on the ground." Olav bent his head and saw a spider on the needle of one juniper.

Between the lichen were small, red flowers. Narrow saplings reached toward the hole above. Some were dead and dried out.

Shilpa stopped in the middle of this almost-round space. "Here we can have a meal break and rest. Look, there is a natural channel, and it has a hole at the end. Can you see? There are two stars to be seen."

"Look at this all," Leevi whispered with surprise. "What a natural temple this is."

"You see that we can make a small fire and maybe dry some humidity from our clothes when we heat something to eat," Shilpa said.

"That would make us fresh human beings again," Leevi said. "I could have never in my wildest dreams imagined this kind of place to be here." He looked at the trees. "These can be very old, even if they are narrow. Life is such a powerful force. With light and humidity, all this is possible. Lichen takes its meal from stones, but I wonder how the nutrition is maintained here for trees and flowers."

He got his answer when they heard a noise near the hole. A herd of Himalayan musk dear jumped over the small hole and, some of their droppings fell down.

The hole was not pointed directly at the sky but tilted at a slight diagonal, for the droppings were dripping on one side of the hole. Now the group understood what the old marks were that they had seen covering one wall of the cliff. All the way down, they'd found their way with the help of some wind and rain that had accelerated this process.

"I'll make the fire now." Olav took dry branches of junipers and dead, slim pines. Carefully, he broke them into small pieces. He took a flat stone and put the material on it. He took smaller stones to build a place for their pot.

"Please wait until I take the ingredients to the pot," Shilpa said as she removed stuff from her rucksack. "We can't waste any heat in case it burns very quickly."

They switched off their lamps and silently ate soup made of different beans and plenty of garlic.

The slice of the sky above them gave them calmness, and the fire heated their cool fingers, noses, and toes.

Soon they had only charcoals left, but they were too tired to worry about that.

"We can try to rest a while here," Shilpa said. "I estimate that we are over the halfway point of our journey." She smiled and took her light but warm sleeping back out from the rucksack. The others followed her example.

"I hope Sophia is well." Olav said aloud their common thought. He also wanted to minimize his phobia and do a favor to the others by lessening their worries of Sophia. He led all to think of something that interested him. "I know that you are all tired, but can you tell me more about reaching pure consciousness according what you have learned?"

"Olav," said Shilpa. "Anyone can do mental practices to reach a level of knowledge where the ultimate reality can be faced. At that level, the universe shows up in its finest form. There is pure consciousness that can be reached in many ways. One way is to say a mantra."

"Okay. What is a mantra in this context?" Olav asked.

Leevi answered. "Basically, a mantra means setting a mind free by using one's voice, which vibrates at the same frequencies as one's mind."

"And does everything that exists have the same frequency according this viewpoint?" Olav asked.

"Good notification." Leevi was proud of Olav as if Olav were his son. "The power behind all beings vibrates in one frequency."

"But what happens to the multitude of beings? Will that disappear?"

Shilpa answered this time. "Each creature vibrates in many frequencies, which in the subtle level are seen in as many colors and hues as there are souls."

"What kind of mantra is nearest to the wholeness?"

"The most important mantra is Aum and the silence that follows it," Shilpa said. "It includes all levels of consciousness: being awake, A; the subconscious, u; the unconscious, m; and in the end, when there is silence, that is pure consciousness."

Leevi reminded them about a not-so-surprising fact. "That very mantra is in many cultures, even if in a changed form. In ancient Egypt, it was Amon; in Buddhism, Aum; in Christianity, amen; in Islam, Alm. If you want, you can try to say it and feel where you sense each sound in your body: Aaaa…Uuuu…Mmm…and silence."

Olav smiled, massaged his left arm, straightened his back, inhaled, and silently made the sounds over and over again. After a while, he stated to Leevi that he felt the A sound more in the middle of his body, the U sound more in the lower part, and the M sound more in the upper part. Silence increased his total relaxation but otherwise was indescribable.

"So, in practice, your whole body is participating in the vibrations of the voice, as well as in silence." Shilpa had quite often felt her body as an instrument, so she could feel Olav's joy.

"And if you now want to, try to say 'amen' slowly. How do you feel?" Leevi asked.

"Are you serious?" Olav laughed but repeated the word slowly. "I felt A more in the middle, M in the upper part of my head, and E more in the area of my neck. N didn't give any special sensations except maybe on the palate, where my tongue pressed."

He considered this a while. "Does this mean that where this word is repeated, the middle and upper parts of the body are more involved, but in a mantra that includes U, the rest of the body vibrates as well?"

"In that way, the whole human body is participating," Shilpa said. "Let's have a broader view of this."

"May I begin?" Leevi asked. He smiled when he rather felt than saw how Shilpa nodded. "If we think how people feel about their religions, we can see that there are differences in emphasizing religion as a more inner or outer experience. I'd say that a more inner personal experience and considering all life to be sacred is one end of the matter. On the other end are cases where people have persecuted and killed others because of what they themselves or others believe. So many warmongers have used religion or faith as an excuse."

"There hasn't been much respect for the possibility to be born as a human being and reach much knowledge and understanding if one so chooses," Shilpa said.

Olav yearned for more knowledge. "I wonder which has a bigger influence prevailing thoughts and thought forms, how a consumer society works by feeding and manipulating or religious ritual behavior."

"I think that any repeated thought, manipulation, or ritual behavior has a huge effect if a person has those thoughts constantly inside his or her head," Leevi said. "Think if you vibrate a certain way daily and even many times per day. That can open you to certain kind of energy more. Your viewpoints can be narrower or broader; what is more, you live your life mostly through that certain level of energy." During his life span Leevi had slowly noticed how much he could affect his own energy.

Olav began to understand. "Like having certain kinds of glasses and hearing tools and certain thought models all the time for observing and understanding and acting."

Shilpa yawned, and Leevi joined her. But Olav became more alarmed when he remembered something. "I`m sure that all this is familiar to you, but could you explain to me why term alchemy is sometimes used in the connection of a human body."

"The terminology was borrowed from the alchemist in the time when development of human being was not free, but one could be burnt or tortured as a witch by the ruling social powers," Leevi said. "But despite the terminology, the question concerns spiritual development of a human being. A human being who wants to make himself or herself indifferent to everything else except the unchangeable is actually carrying out inner alchemy using the self as a tool and laboratory. What he or she can find behind the changeable is 'gold,' the unchangeable truth."

"What is the process?" Olav asked.

"A person goes through human powers in his or her own body and recognizes them so they don't rule him or her. What is more, no one else can rule him or her with their help. Only a human's self is a master of his or her own powers." Leevi thought that he couldn't emphasize this enough.

"What sort of powers do you mean?" Olav was like a sponge sucking the water of information.

"The elementary powers in a human being are all the universal states: feelings, desires, and an endless stream of thoughts. Images rise up with the moods that a human being experiences." Leevi had done practices with these.

"And what is the result of the process?"

"When a human being finally knows his or her own powers, he or she is a newborn, in a way. The elementary powers are loosened into a universal liquid, and then they are allowed to come back as refined. After that, a spirit manifests consciously in such a way that a human consciousness is no longer outside the consciousness of the universe. The human being has assimilated that knowledge. Then, there is only one whole consciousness." Leevi's voice was humble.

Shilpa contributed. "The assimilation with the universe can also happen when you keep mind, intentions, and actions pure. At first, temporarily, one can reach the target in silent meditation. When we live in the world, life situations will be real tests for our own powers." Shilpa remembered her own path and how the process took time and effort.

"What do you mean by a real test?" Olav was on the road, but had he understood the traffic marks?

"You must be able to have an attitude and reaction in life situations where your own powers are like trained horses rather than wild ones," Shilpa said.

"Then your body is an instrument of pure energy that plays pure notes."

"Also, it means that the aura is so purified that there is no longer material that colorizes or twists the truth." Leevi knew that this could be possible after disciplined training.

There had been silence for quite a while, but one issue tortured Olav. "And are there setbacks if one doesn't manage to keep up the process till the final goal?"

Shilpa whispered. "Then the reality is still colorized and twisted. Accordingly, that affects attitudes, actions, thoughts, and feelings. The circle continues by piling karma and facing it in this or another life."

"If I have understood correctly, willpower and truthfulness are very good abilities to process oneself," Olav said.

"Yes, indeed," said Leevi. "And I would add a search for an inspiring, high-level energy in beauty, wisdom, music, and nature. But remember, when you analyze after going as far as possible with reason, listen to the silence. Our gifts are many: the observation system and mind serve a human being to become a self-conscious being who can express and scrutinize oneself. Then how far one can develop depends on the will that rules one's own energies. To me, the only death is ignorance, and life means knowledge." Leevi was grateful that he could give some hints to Olav, who seemed to be growing all the time.

"Is that knowledge possible to anyone?" Olav asked.

"Sure, when one begins to search for truth with devotion," Shilpa said.

"Life can be lived without a profound knowledge," said Leevi. "And suddenly, one can awaken from ignorance, the only real death, and learn about one's own spirituality—in other words, to become alive. In this process, one believes at first that only a body that is observable with bare eyes is all." Leevi remembered such phases in his own life.

"I have had two ways of understanding life," Olav said. "Part of me believed that only the body is all, and part believed that spirituality is somewhere outside me." He drank some water after this confession.

"That seems to be a very natural process; when we get used to the body, we use senses to observe everything outside us," Leevi said. "Then, later, we can realize that to reach the inner source of wisdom, we need to take the attention there, too. If one thinks far enough about how all works and is maintained, there must arise a question of something very intelligent in this all. Most people are in the process of increasing consciousness. Being too judgmental even toward oneself would only keep the awareness down." Leevi had seen many situations in life and kept his hopes high. "Through insights and practices or experiences, in many lives, this 'dead stone'—a developing human being—changes himself or herself into a living 'wisdom stone.'"

"What is the role of energy centers, according these concepts?" Something tickled Olav's chest, and he had to change the position of his hands, which were under his head, to be able to scratch.

Shilpa answered. "Energy centers are connected with all that is in human beings. How open they are reveals the energy level of a person. In the case of waking up and noticing one's own spirituality, a human being can begin to develop his or her energy centers purposefully in his or her own subtle body. The best way is to develop the so-called heart center in the middle of the chest first to experience the unity of all beings." Shilpa's eyes wondered to the hole high above, where a single star was.

"Yes, it is empathy, which is a key to truths!" Leevi turned his face toward Olav in the dim light that came from the narrow channel.

Olav's profile looked like a shadow. "Are there serious dangers in developing and opening of one's own energies?"

"The real danger is that if powerful energies open without the truth and wisdom of the heart, they can be strongly twisted and colorized according to a prevailing thought and feeling that a person happens to have." Shilpa knew exactly what she spoke about. She'd intensively felt all her feelings once she could begin to devote her energy to spiritual practices. Her children became adults almost at the same time when her dear husband left this world. Then a more intensive phase for her spiritual growth began.

"Despite a danger, I am sure that many will still long for and even cry for developing during one lifetime," Leevi said. "I mean, who wouldn't?" He understood that many people could live their lives without reaching turning points that could wake them to search for truth. But some were more open to search even without big crises that shook their lives. "That is a built-in attraction, such as between magnetic matters, and the closer someone is to the goal, the bigger is the longing toward it."

Shilpa continued. "Nevertheless, without the first energy center, others wouldn't get enough strength to open up properly. That is why issues connected with safety and survival have to be dealt with. In so doing, one builds up a base to consciously let more powerful energies stream through one's body."

Leevi nodded. "The nervous system must be strong, and the body must be durable, so a very strong creative power that will awaken from this first center in its full strength won't destroy the body when it will be lifted up through all the main energy centers." Leevi had been doing some practices daily to keep his body in good condition.

"So, Olav," Shilpa said. "You understand that one's own body is a tool and instrument vitally important for a fully conscious human being. Being born as a human being is a privilege and a sacred matter. No one should ever take that possibility from anyone or oneself, either."

Leevi looked at Olav's face in the darkness. "One warning I still have to say. Do not try to open your full energies too early before you are mentally ready.

The destruction would be like a lightning strike to a transformer when the conductors are not suitable. One can die or become paralyzed. Patience and self-discipline are great human abilities."

"And when the energies open more, what do they bring along?" Olav asked.

"Now, when a human develops oneself in one's own body, he or she develops in this process and reaches the possibility to understand and observe matters and objects that were invisible before," Shilpa said.

"Invisible! Do you mean matters that can be seen with a microscope or radiation or ultrasound?" Olav felt invisible in the darkness, but in daylight it would be a strange feeling.

"Not exactly, but it's true that one can know his or her own physical body, too." Shilpa moved her legs to keep her toes warm. "To notice new levels in consciousness is part of one's development, anyway; we cannot see our thoughts, either, even if they fill our mind or feelings, even if they arouse moods in us. We just realize how they manifest in behavior and actions. It is important that one is aware of these energies and notices in oneself joyful moments and depressive moments, then one sees his or her qualities."

"One faces situations, which arouse feelings," Leevi said. "Then, little by little, one understands how these arose from the attitude one has. That is what one can effect on and practice then, and it helps control feelings. One can also do practices in which one's awareness can be broadened when one produces moods without causes and identifies oneself with them, as well as chooses not to identify with them. Then the control over them would be won."

"What about being captured in one energy level?" Olav thought that such a case would be common.

"Everything can be taken to the extreme, like endless gormandizing," Leevi said. "It's also difficult not to attach to results and targets; with gluttony, there are endless routes for that." Leevi considered that they lived in a world where it was too easy to jail oneself. "Nothing is enough, and that causes continuous dissatisfaction. Staying alert and honest to oneself is a way to maintain a free outlook."

Olav had more questions. "Do you mean that, if one cannot be moderate, one can be captured in one energy level? But if one keeps one's energies moving and does not stop to overeat with any feeling or thought, one stays awake and alert and as a part of all energies? Isn't it just feelings that differentiate a human being from a machine?"

"Yes, it's amazing to feel," said Leevi. "But being caught by a feeling would be like meeting a person who would lock you in just to have that one feeling." Leevi supposed that having a low-level feeling forever would be a real hell.

"Joy seems to influence a person so one becomes revived and feels healthier when depression could otherwise paralyze him or her like a poison." Olav had observed himself especially after his divorce.

"Now, we need to think about the vibrational frequencies of feelings," Leevi said. "Joy is high, and bliss is even higher, whereas grief has a low frequency. Both manifest as feelings." He had always been thrilled by the mechanics of these energies.

"An expression of higher energies, like bliss, has a good effect, even on one's surroundings," Shilpa said. Her toes were warm again, and she felt sleepier.

"The last question now, I promise," said Olav, already keeping his eyes closed and feeling a bit uncomfortable on the hard surface of the cave. "Do you know people who managed to reach the ultimate development of a human being and maintain it?"

"Difficult to say for sure," Shilpa said. "After all, it's inner development. But what one can say about the fruits of action or behavior is that there have been spiritual teachers whose teachings may be twisted after their death." Shilpa pondered about the difference between individual inner experience and institutionalized instructions. "I do not name anyone, but difficulties can begin when an association, institution, or group tries to maintain truthfulness together. One can demand from oneself, but the same matter can arouse misunderstandings and different interpretations when discussed in a group and demanded from others."

Leevi nodded in the darkness. "There have been several so-called trials of utopian societies round the world. For example, one of my ancestors went to Canada to participate in establishing a community in

Malcolm island. Those trials didn't last long as ideal, but to have the whole world as one team might require a catastrophe for a common goal. Good routes to increase benevolence are sport and culture happenings, where competition and sharing can be in a playful way."

"What are you saying? Why have trials of dream societies ended?" Olav asked.

"If one is not careful, one often asks from others more than from oneself," Leevi said. "Also, envy and jealousy can be glasses that one doesn't notice easily on his or her own nose. People tend to make comparisons between each other. It is all about selfishness. An unselfish society needs unselfish individuals, but people are on different phases in their own path. It is rare to notice entirely pure energy." Leevi wanted to sleep, but one thing had to be clarified. "This might also be an issue about how low and high energies move among people."

"How do they move? Can't one affect them?" Olav felt peaceful when he saw a piece of open sky in the middle of the darkness. Somewhere high up, a lonely cloud crossed the sky, covering the starlight.

"We have so many thoughts and feelings around in the level of manifestation among crowds," Leevi said. "Many of those usually have lower frequencies, such as worries, sadness, depression, hate, and irritation."

"That sounds reasonable." Olav thought how he'd got used to such energies as they were the norm.

"If there is any small spot of those kinds of feelings or thoughts in a person, that spot in him or her tends to get bigger easily among a crowd," Leevi said.

"Do you mean that the special content of a thought or feeling would spread around?" Olav raised his eyebrows in disbelief.

"No, dear Olav," Leevi said. "Only the level of frequencies. But we all have matters and people to which we might connect them."

"Are there any ways to avoid that?" Olav was embarrassed thinking that he must have experienced that a lot. He'd been provoked by many kinds of feelings.

"Again, be aware of that process. Only if you do not have any spot of those qualities in your energy field can you wander anywhere and waves of energies that are not in your aura won't attach. Also remember that your own thoughts, what you cherish and cultivate, surround you always and reach you first when you begin a silent moment."

"So a person with pure energy doesn't fall anymore?"

"Even then, one can begin to collect low level energies if one chooses so. We have free will. But then when you have more energy, your expressions are more impressive, and those feelings and thoughts are more powerful than in a person whose energies are not so open. What is more, low energies will take you lower than people who haven't opened access to their energies." Leevi had often felt the possibility to choose in life situations. He'd chosen goodness consciously and resisted with willpower a possibility to do bad. He knew people who were generally ethical in actions but had chosen to use alcohol or drugs; lost their willpower, even if temporarily; and justified themselves through those inhuman choices.

"Will that kind of person lose all acquired awareness, understanding, and skills?" Olav shivered in the cold. He tucked himself better in the sleeping bag and pressed his back against Leevi's back.

"Indeed, he or she will, and it'll be more difficult to rise up again." Leevi's circulation was good. He felt like a battery who heated their unique sleeping space.

"I would recommend periods of purification in peaceful surroundings to diminish lower energies and to increase and maintain higher ones," Shilpa said.

"Do you suggest a certain period in a year?" Olav mumbled under his sleeping bag.

"There can be longer periods at any time of the year, preferable spent near nature. Shorter periods, I recommend on a daily basis. They keep a person alert and more conscious of his or her own inner state." Shilpa had lived a while like that.

"Being constantly aware and alert and taking time off daily plus longer periods during a year is the way to sail on the energy sea toward a broader understanding and awareness." Olav repeated his statement in order to remember it.

"Yes," said Shilpa. "To me, a very good rule is to follow good ethics toward oneself and others, take care of the body with exercises, breathe the energy with consciousness, and regularly let the attention go inside one's own mind. Once there, concentrate, meditate, and let the higher level affect you."

Leevi yawned and closed his eyes. "Ethics is the core of any human behavior to reach oneness and celebrate life as a human being, as well as to let others celebrate it, too. But now, let's have some sleep."

Through the mountain tunnels and channels came a distant, constant noise. "Like a drill," Shilpa whispered aloud. "No, it can't be."

CHAPTER TWENTY

Olav, Shilpa, and Leevi were all exhausted. The steps to the rocky corridor, where they saw open sky again, had been difficult. They hadn't slept much, and their eyes were tired. Bright light blinded them at first. The rock ceiling was partly above them, but there was a hole big enough for a human being to go in or out. To Shilpa's horror, it appeared to have been used a lot.

She saw clear marks made by boots; some litter from rucksacks; a regularly used fireplace with cooking possibility; a small tent that housed a sleeping bag and boxes filled with sample cases, a microscope, test tubes…

"Look at this!" she said. "What a shame! Who has been here? What is happening here? Rajan, my son, what have you done? My worst fear has come true; some ignorant travelers have found the place of my family or were led here on purpose. Hurry! We have to stop this." She rushed forward and began to run.

Olav and Leevi had also noticed the place and were worried for Shilpa, as well as Sophia.

"This can't be Sophia's doing," Leevi said.

Olav nodded. "Will Shilpa believe us?"

"She will when we reach the person who really has been doing all this. I just wonder what he's been searching for." Leevi's face was serious with concentration. "Are there valuable metals or stones here?"

"We'll learn that soon. Can you run?"

"Sure, at my own speed. Please, you run after Shilpa and help her if necessary." Leevi followed Olav slowly to mind his steps.

Olav tried to speed up, but he noticed the ceiling was getting lower once again, so he had crawl. It was dark; his headlamp was with Shilpa. Leevi came behind and needed his own lamp. Olav felt terrible claustrophobia this time. Alone in the darkness and crawling in a black hole, he could sense all the walls around him literally.

He concentrated on breathing slowly. He began to count each movement that he made with his hands and legs. "One, two…" One hand, one leg in its own time. He saw Sophia's face in his mind, and his movements became more relaxed and strong. After what seemed to be an hour, he saw light ahead. He pulled himself quietly out of the low corridor and crawled behind a big stone to check the situation.

Shilpa was saying something to a small, muscular, dark-haired man who stood with a drill in his hands. "In what right have you come to disturb the peace of this place?" she asked.

Leo stared at her as if she were an alien from a different planet. "I could ask you the same." He slowly placed the drill on the ground. He wiped his hands on his black trousers, which were covered in brown and white dust. He wore a T-shirt that had maybe once been white. He continued with an angry voice. "Who the hell are you? What is this traffic in such a remote place?"

"What traffic? Have you seen a young woman?" Shilpa was suddenly more alert.

"Sure, I'll show you." Leo changed his tone and approached Shilpa in order to take a grip of her arm.

Olav jumped from his hiding place. "And show that to me, too!" His voice was hard, and adrenaline streamed through his body.

"And who is this knight?" Leo asked. "Come along. And you, too. Yes, you behind the stone, you with white hair." Leevi entered. Leo addressed the group. "I see I'm outnumbered. But this will equalize the situation." He reached into the side pocket of his trousers and produced a gun.

"Please do not use that," said Shilpa. "We'll all be buried here because of the noise that makes." Shilpa was thinking of Sophia, Olav, and Leevi. Why did I tell anyone of this place? she pondered. She'd jeopardized these people by telling the secret to Rajan and Sophia and by leading Leevi and Olav here. "Did Rajan tell you about this place?" She had to restrain her voice.

"Or was it your dear, precious Sophia?" Leo laughed. "Maybe it was her. Women tend to be weak and untrustworthy." He saw that his words had some impact on Shilpa, so he continued. "One needs only to look at you, Aunt Shilpa. You have told your big secret to everyone. How else would we all be here now? You carry the responsibility if we all are buried here." He laughed and aimed the gun at her.

Before he could shoot, Olav and Leevi jumped in the way. Astonished, Leo missed his target; instead, the bullet hit Olav's right leg. Stones began to fall. Leo escaped to the narrow tunnel from where the others had crawled earlier.

"What's happening there?" Sophia's voice sounded as if it were coming from a well.

Shilpa seemed to know where to go and waved Leevi and Olav to follow her. They managed to avoid the bigger stones that fell, but their hair was filled with small ones and dust.

When they reached the small space where Sophia was, they noticed that she'd been struck on her head, evidently by a falling stone. Shilpa checked Sophia's pulse and pupils. Olav and Leevi found suitable stones to hit the metal chains that attached Sophia to the granite wall.

"Drills are dangerous in silly hands," Olav said. "Why has he captured her like this?" Olav wondered about the twisted imagination of the man they'd just met.

Finally, they got Sophia free, but they still had to find a way out of the place, which was falling apart.

"And how is your leg, big boy?" Shilpa asked and griped Olav's leg with her skillful hands. "The bullet has to be removed, but it has to wait until we are in a more stable place. You all will now learn the second route from here. Maybe then the secret hasn't any meaning anymore. I have a feeling that the legend has been fulfilled and the place will be hidden forever."

Leevi wiped dust from his face. "Shilpa, if we find a way out of here, I wish that you'll come visit Sophia's home village."

"It is a deal," Shilpa prayed silently in her mind that they all wouldn't end their lives inside this mountain.

Once again the men followed Shilpa. Leevi carried Sophia, even though Olav wanted to. He didn't think much of the wound on his leg. After a while, they had to kneel and crawl into a narrow tunnel.

"Let's make a sledge from a sleeping bag and fill it with other sleeping bags to increase the softness against the hard, stony ground," Shilpa said.

Leevi pulled and Olav pushed the soft sledge, where Sophia rested like a baby. Sometimes she moaned weakly that they could let her out, which they considered as a good sign. She was back with them, but Shilpa wanted her to rest, so she was stuck.

This time inside the tunnel, Olav was so worried about Sophia that he forgot to think about the walls all around him. Perhaps he conquered his phobia.

They could hear a rumbling sound as they exited the narrow, black tunnel and entered a big space. One of the walls was rushing water. Morning had broken through the waterfall, and the first rays of the rising sun dazzled their eyes, which were not used to such brightness.

"We are here," Sophia said. "Isn't this place beautiful? Thank you for rescuing me! I can understand that Shilpa and Olav came after me, but Grandfather, how have you joined them? Shouldn't you be above the Arctic Circle planting potatoes?" Sophia smiled through tears.

She turned to Olav. "Olav, have you tuned your brain waves?" She reminded him of their old discussions.

"Sure I have. We need to compare our experiences. I have a feeling that you might have shared one or two waves with me." Olav was smiling but had serious eyes. "How is your head? Do you feel nausea?"

"Do not begin with that. It is enough that Aunt Shilpa fusses."

"Now," Shilpa said. "We have to check your wound, Olav. Maybe I can remove the bullet here. And do not look at me like that; I happen to have some stuff for local anesthetics…Unless you prefer hypnosis?"

Leevi had gone through the waterfall. He came back totally wet, looked at them, and laughed. "I am so happy that we reached here, but you don't seem worried about we'll get down to the valley."

He continued in a more serious manner. "Was it really Leo who drilled there and shot at Olav? He said 'Aunt Shilpa.' Shilpa, have you met him before accidently?"

"Were there any branches outside so that we can make a fire and heat some water for Olav's leg?" Shilpa had ignored his question. He would have to wait for her answer a lot longer than any of them imagined.

Leevi went back out. Later, he returned with some dry branches which he tried to protect from waterfall.

Shilpa looked at Olav's leg. "You were so lucky that it wasn't an exploding bullet. I got it out and sewed up the wound. It will be as good as new." She rose to her feet. "Is the soup hot, Leevi?"

She got a steaming bowl in her hands and had nearly finished the last drops of soup when they all heard a noise that penetrated the roaring waterfall.

Leevi hurried to check and soon rushed back. "It's a helicopter. A green helicopter is flying round the ledge. It has a rope ladder swinging under it. Could it be anyone you know?" he asked with a smile.

Shilpa left her bowl on the ground. Outside, she saw Rajan poke his head out from the flying vehicle.

Rajan shouted over the noise. "Hello, folks! Do you mind using a rope ladder?"

Shilpa waved to him, happy at this unexpected turning point. She'd prayed and hoped and told herself to trust her son.

Rajan had made his choice. Shilpa was almost sure that the expensive, luxury things at home were not mere acquisitions but a result of Leo's arrival at the mountain. She was angry but also proud, for Rajan had come to rescue them after all. He was surely a complex son, but they had a bond of affection. "You are joking about using rope ladders, right?" she shouted to him.

Leevi and Shilpa carefully carried all the rucksacks and helped Sophia and Olav to the other side of the roaring waterfall.

Soon, several rope ladders were swinging wildly in front of them. While the helicopter hovered in one place, the group climbed up. Shilpa, who avoided looking down from the moving ladders, climbed with Olav. He needed less help because of his strong arms. He enjoyed the wind on his face. Slightly weak, Sophia climbed slowly up with Leevi, smiling. Leevi's blue eyes marveled at the snowy mountaintops all around. Far below pines moved in the wind, and he could smell their familiar fragrance.

EPILOGUE

Sophia took another sapling from the basket that hung over her shoulder. "I must admit that the trip to find my biological roots resulted in much more broader viewpoints than I could ever have hoped for."

Olav nodded. "I couldn't agree more. I was quite confused before the trip, and now I can formulate that while we approached our target to rescue you, I was on a journey inside myself. I would have not expected to have the pleasure of being accompanied by two human beings as wise as Shilpa and Leevi."

Shilpa smiled. "We have learned in our turn from people who carried out their spiritual journey on the earth. With opening to truth, a human being really reveals that a person is a mask, as the original meaning of that word describes. Through a person, a mask, pure consciousness can appear to anyone."

Leevi put another small pine on the ground. "There you say words of wisdom. The purer the feelings, thoughts, and intentions are, the more a human being can observe and affect his or her surroundings. We can be joyful if some light has shined through us. More light is the purpose of anyone who reaches in oneself." He used his boot to press the soil around the pine. 'We didn't have time to talk much in Nepal due to some urgent matters concerning Sophia's and Olav's injures. Then, my and Olav's visas were getting old, and we had to travel before meeting you here. Not that I complain. As you saw yesterday, we'd prepared my farmhouse and serpent-spruce cottage in a costume celebration for you."

All smiled at the memories. Shilpa recalled two surprises vividly…

They faced with the first one when they arrived by Sophia's small, dark-blue electric car to Leevi's farmhouse: Leevi's neighbors welcomed them with a garden party.

The local farmers' wives association helped Leevi provide local treats. Tables outside were filled with fresh salads of tomatoes, cucumbers, and lettuce from Leevi's own greenhouse. Local fish that Olav proudly claimed to have caught was been grilled along with potatoes, carrots, and edible varieties of turnip. Shilpa enjoyed the food, especially after Sophia brought her extra chili and garlic.

The taste of the forest included blueberry, lingonberry, and cloudberry pies served with vanilla ice cream. Shilpa noticed the rather sour aroma but was grateful for the sweet ice cream.

A group of local musicians provided beautiful singing and brisk dancing. Shilpa had learned the steps of jenkka, a Finnish folk dance, which had been her late sister's favorite in her youth.

Shilpa and Sophia walked inside Leevi's red, wooden farmhouse with a big porch. They went through an old cattle shelter and a barn, which were just opposite the house. Some rowan trees were flowering in white, giving shade to the left side of the house, while a pine forest towered to the right and behind the house.

The two women went inside to a cozy living room. Sophia asked Shilpa to sit in a wooden rocking chair with red-yellow, soft cover. She had shown old photos to Shilpa. It had been touching. Shilpa had realized that in that very chair, Silja had rocked a very young Sophia. Shilpa closed her eyes and opened them again, imagining how children had grown here. Two colorful, wool handicrafts on the wall captured her attention. One described the dazzling colors of autumn, whereas the other gave an impression of the powerfully radiating Northern Lights. Leevi had mentioned that his late wife had woven them. Two wooden sofas were lined up next to the windows, which had warm, yellow curtains. In the kitchen corner, a big, wooden table was covered with white linen, and some white cups were on it. Shilpa considered that the heart of that room was a huge stove. Leevi had heated it since he baked some rieska—traditional, thin, unleavened bread made from barley. Shilpa had loved it. Near the stove, on a chair, was a black cat, which Leevi had called Missu. Her watery-green eyes followed their every movement.

Later, Leevi walked with Shilpa by the shiny, blue lake, which was visible between the cattle house and the barn all the way to the front door of the house. They let Sophia and Olav take an old rowboat that had waited on the beach. Shilpa and Leevi had been satisfied to sit on the bench under the fragrant birches that lead toward the wavy water. But they hadn't had too many peaceful moments because everybody wanted to talk with Sophia's newly found aunt.

The second surprise was revealed after Leevi and Olav asked the women to take only the very necessary stuff for being outdoors overnight. Then Leevi gave a small speech.

"The last time we met, we spent most of the time inside and on the slopes of a huge mountain. Sophia happens to have a license to fly, and we have our small, electrically charged airplane in a shelter behind the house. You women can be birds for a while. You, Shilpa, our trusted guide of the Himalayas, are the one who deserves a proper view over Sophia's and Your late sister's childhood landscape."

Shilpa laughed with delight. "What about you? Will you hang below us with the help of rope ladders?"

Everybody applauded, waiting to see a kind of circus. But Olav commented. "We surely would if the airplane were powerful enough for our extra weight. But this time, we're satisfied with another vehicle."

Leevi had walked to the side of his house during the general noise, and now he returned with two rucksacks and a red moped, along with two yellow helmets. "That is even better!" some of the neighbors said...

Sophia still felt the excitement of their flight. "The airplane was such a joy to handle. You should have seen my aunt's face when we rose up over the lake and the tops of pine forest. A grey-white owl flew momentarily on our side."

"Inside the airplane, we did feel like eagles for a while," Shilpa said. "It was surely different from flying in a jet. Everything was so much nearer the trees, small ponds, and swamps. I saw a brown bear with her cubs. From far away, I still recognized a point that was the roof of your house, Leevi. Even the lake was like a tiny puddle. The wooden, two-storied cottage is such a pearl. It's just like what you told me in Nepal. The curved spruce trunks still head upward; they were even more impressive than I imagined. Sophia said that when you started to build the cottage, you found four big, white quartz stones and used them as cornerstones. They made me feel that part of the holy, secret place—which Sophia reached to see before it was buried—is here. It maybe always has been." Shilpa smiled. A lot of light shimmered in her black eyes, which looked acceptingly into Leevi's sky-blue eyes.

Leevi sported a broad smile. "Holiness is found everywhere, but only an open heart feels it. The whole world is a miracle, although I am pleased that you felt the magic of the cottage."

Shilpa laughed. "By the way, I enjoyed the sauna a lot. When I sat with Sophia round the fireplace, it was very relaxing. Sorry that we were so tired that we went to sleep before you arrived from the sauna. All the wonderful happenings of that day helped me sleep, even if the sun seemed to be out all night and into the morning." Shilpa supposed that getting used to the sunlight at night would take a while.

'Yes. It's not possible to admire the Milky Way in summer. But when you come in autumn, you'll see that along with the Northern Lights. Then the sun is maybe too low."

Shilpa narrowed her eyes. "Where did you hide your moped? I didn't see it in the morning."

'It is waiting for us like a faithful, old horse by one very wet swamp," Olav said. "We had to leave the moped to continue by walking in wet shoes. That is why we were so glad that you two had put enough firewood in the sauna's oven and we could go directly there. Thank you for the soup that you left for us. Its garlic and beans vividly reminded me of our wandering in tunnels and caves. We didn't want to wake you up too early, considering your jet lag."

"No worries," Sophia said. "I did know the way to this planting area. You two are workaholics. But see how quick we have been since we participated in planting." She teased and waved toward the lines of saplings.

They continued planting till Leevi called them to gather round an old fireplace. "Here we make a fire. Is the water pot in your rucksack, Olav? Have you heard anything about Leo, Sophia? I wonder what happened to him."

Olav passed a pot to Leevi. "Here it is." He and Shilpa began to collect old branches.

Sophia found old, dry pinecones and put them on the fireplace. "No, I haven't. I just wonder how the legend took place concerning him. He was there but didn't experience the opening of his energies. Many times, I wondered why he didn't mention the extraordinary place at all. He'd found that route, too, but only hatred had increased in him. Maybe, as I experienced it, the treasure inside the mountain could be interpreted as a script about the growth of a human being toward a conscious, creative being who knows his own and others' energies. That seems to be for those who are ready to understand its meaning. The effect of the cave strengthened the energies that are dominant in a person."

Leevi poured pure water in the pot. "Oh, indeed. Only an unselfish person whose energies are resonating with it enough could understand its meaning. How brilliant and logical! Your energies were pure!" Leevi looked at her and was happy that she was back home.

"And what happened to Rajan, Shilpa?" Leevi took rieska slices, cheese, salted salmon, tomatoes, and boiled eggs from his rucksack. Shilpa shrugged. Leevi thought about how much worry Rajan had caused her.

Shilpa took one egg and began to peel it. "When I think of him, I know that he seems to live at a crossroad. Sometimes he uses energy that helps him toward broader consciousness, but from time to time he uses energy that represents greed and ignorance. I try to help him in my thoughts and words by believing and strengthening the good in him. I know that all his choices are his, and he finds justification in whatever he decides."

Leevi admired her. "You are a wonderful mother and human being! When situations come and he thinks of you, your encouragement and trust will support him to make choices that lift him up and broaden his views."

"It's true that the resonance is stronger between genetically similar people," said Olav, who had listened in. He added butter and cheese on his rieska slice. "But as I experienced with you, higher thoughts and feelings seem to reproduce even between nonrelatives, too. All women and men have the same tools, indeed. Our wandering inside that mountain was like spending some time inside our own brains and, in addition, the whole observable and subtle body."

Shilpa looked at the two younger persons. "Olav and Sophia, you both were so ready, like matured fruits, for reaching a new level as human beings. Even if you had different approaching views, you reached the same level." She felt so blessed that Sophia had found her and spurred the expedition with Leevi and Olav.

Here the mountains were not very high; they had worn down millions of years ago. But they offered a stable ground for spruces and pines and some safe hiding places for wild animals. They also offered good scenery, such as the one where the group now rested. Under the arctic summer sun, they felt grateful for the mild, southwest breeze that carried fragrances. The slight smell of pines gave way to the birches that celebrated their prime time, and their freshness was almost intoxicating. Greenness embraced the group as if Mother Earth herself had surrounded them by miracles of growing and new birth.

Leevi turned to Sophia. "Why do you think, Sophia, that we have abilities to feel endless like the universe in our consciousness?" A cap shaded Sophia's eyes, and they appeared dark and bottomless with single stars in each, reflecting the sun's rays off a metal spoon in her mug.

"I think that we are an organic part of all the matter, dark matter, and dark energy. We also have mass and nonmass in us. When we know ourselves, we are able to experience profoundly everything in us." Sophia's eyes were filled with warm light as she lifted her chin up toward the sun.

Olav smiled. "What makes mankind unique is that we literally have all the levels of consciousness, including subconsciousness and supraconsciousness, to reach all existing knowledge and wisdom." He narrowed his eyes to Shilpa, who nodded.

"I have pondered how people who misuse their energies to harm others in fact harm themselves most, since we are all connected and in interaction," she said. "How wise and purposeful is the karma when souls need to face what they caused and then go further with bigger wisdom sooner or later. A human being is a participant in this complicated existence through feelings and thoughts and, above all, through a direction of one's own consciousness." Shilpa looked to a meadow on their right side.

Yellow globeflowers were blossoming; their mild, fine smell moved with the wind. Different serenades of birds touched their hearts. Olav recognized a robin and a finch, as well as the very distant voice of a cuckoo. A gray-white reindeer with her small calf passed the human group.

Leevi wanted to describe the big change he'd seen growing in Olav. "Olav, you have reached the hidden, forgotten part of yourself and have lost the ignorance concerning your origin and inner secrets. You are aware of a light in you now, not only matter. Olav, you have changed more toward valo, or light."

"That can be so." Olav smiled peacefully. "What about you, Sophia, the chosen one of your family?"

"Sure, I can honestly say that I understand why Einstein imagined that he traveled on a ray of light," Sophia said. "And I've read stories about how Milarepa, a great yogi, flew with one. But I identify myself sometimes with a resting photon, having no mass whatsoever."

Sophia continued with enthusiasm. "Now I also realize perfectly what the circles inside each other meant. It's about connecting a conscious energy in many minds at the same time. That is a power that pushes a change to a broader level. In time, it will make the whole of mankind reach ethical heights, a more truthful and responsible way to live as a creating part of wholeness. We are all chosen."

The End